Curriculum Materials Collection
Ratner Media Center
2030 South Taylor Road
Cleveland Heights, Ohio 44118

CMC	Glicksberg, Abraham A.
236.4	Educational values in
GLI	the shulchan aruch
2299	c.1

Educational Values in the Shulchan Aruch

by
Abraham A. Glicksberg

SHENGOLD PUBLISHERS
New York

This book is based on my doctoral dissertation. At the recommendation of friends in the field of Jewish education, I have extracted those parts of my study which are useful to the Jewish educator and to the general reader interested in the traditional values of Jewish education.

ISBN 0-88400-105-9
Library of Congress Catalog Card Number: 84-50678
Copyright © 1984 by Abraham A. Glicksberg

All rights reserved

Published by Shengold Publishers, Inc.
New York, N.Y.

Printed in the United States of America

CONTENTS

Preface vii
Introduction ix
Chapter I: Joseph Caro and the Background of the Shulchan Aruch .. 1
  1. The Shulchan Aruch 1
  2. Joseph Caro 4
  3. The Jewish Community in Turkey in Caro's Time 6
  4. The Jewish Community in Palestine in Caro's Time 10
Chapter II: The Basic Educational Principles and Practices in the Shulchan Aruch 14
  1. Physical Development: Rest, Health and Hygiene, Food, Recreation 14
  2. Moral and Ethical Development 17
  3. Arousing Interest and Stimulating Effort 17
  4. Learning by Doing—Directed Activity and Self Activity 18
  5. Individual Differences 20
  6. Memory 20
  7. Inculcation of Right Conduct 21
  8. Social Development 23
  9. Respect for Parents and Respect for Teachers and Elders 23
  10. Training for Leadership, Lay Leadership 24
  11. Responsibility to the Community 25
  12. Respect for Historical Events 26
  13. Maintaining the Religious Spirit 26
  14. Social Adjustment Between Jews and Non-Jews 27
  15. Jewish Attitude Towards Government 29
  16. Attitude Towards Secular Studies 29
  17. Educational Practices in the Shulchan Aruch 29
  18. Early Childhood Education 29
  19. The Basic Curriculum 30
  20. Home 30
  21. Intensity of Learning 30

22. Classroom Discipline 31
23. The Slow Learner 31
24. The Learning Process 31
25. The Teacher 32
26. Adult Education 34
27. The Education of Women 34

Chapter III: Analysis of the Basic Educational Principles and Practices in the Shulchan Aruch in Relation to Modern Education 35
1. Physical Development: Rest, Health and Hygiene, Food and Recreation 35
2. Arousing Interest and Stimulating Effort 36
3. Learning by doing—Self Activity 36
4. Individual Differences 36
5. Memory 37
6. Inculcation of Right Conduct 37
7. Social Development 37
8. Respect for Parents, Teachers and Elders 37
9. Training for Leadership 37
10. Responsibilty to the Community 38
11. Respect for Histroical Events 38
12. Social Adjustment Between Jews and Non-Jews 38
13. Jewish Attitude Towards Government 38
14. Attitude Towards Secular Studies 38
15. Educational Practices 39
16. Early Childhood Education 39
17. The Basic Curiculum 39
18. Intensity of Learning 39
19. Size of Class 39
20. Classroom Discipline 40
21. The Slow Learner 40
22. The Book—Tool of Learning 40
23. The Learning Process 40
24. The Teacher 40
25. Adult Education 41
26. The Education of Women 41

Chapter IV: The Sources of Joseph Caro's Educational Ideas 42

Chapter V: The Relation of the Shulchan Aruch to Later Theories and Practices
of Jewish Education 52
1. Introductory Note..................................... 52
2. Recognition of the Shulchan Aruch in the Seventeenth Century . 52
3. The Status of the Shulchan Aruch in Poland and Russia 52
4. The Shulchan Aruch as a Subject of Study 53
5. The Status of the Shulchan Aruch in Other European Countries . 54
6. TheStudy of the Shulchan Aruch from the Eighteenth Century On ..
56
7. Introductory Note..................................... 56
8. Poland, Rumania, Hungary, England, Israel, Morocco, Canada 56

Chapter VI: The Shulchan Aruch—Its Significance in the Past—Its Educational Contents—Its Recent Status 69

Notes 73

PREFACE

Dr. Abraham Glicksberg is both an accomplished scholar and an exemplary teacher of Judaism and Hebrew. But above all, he is a very good man. He has done most of his teaching not in the Yeshivah world, but in the far more hostile context of the secular university system. The contrast and tension between these two very different educational systems is explicitly one of the main themes of this book. Dr. Glicksberg has described some of his experiences in both worlds and some of his thoughts on Judaism in *Come Back Jewish Youth Come Back Home* (Shengold Publishers, 1983) to which I was honored to add an introduction. The present book is an edited version of Dr. Glicksberg's Ph.D. thesis at New York University, *Educational Principles and Practices in the Shulchan Aruch*.

In Judaism, education, religious observance, and everyday business practice and personal behavior are not separate domains. Jewish law encompasses every area of life of the whole Jewish community. Because of this, Jewish education does not concentrate on imparting a certain level of vocational skills, cultural information, and citizenship characteristics to the young, although these are important. Rather, it is an ongoing lifetime process, in which learning is inextricably wedded to action. Since what is learned is to be practiced, and indeed since learning itself is one of the practices, there is no need for outside inducements. There are no tests in this world, no grades, no degrees (in the secular sense). Education is student oriented: the slow student must practice too. Also, if curriculum means that some subjects have to be "covered" over a given period of time, while other subjects cannot be discussed, there is also no curriculum. Any Torah-related question deserves an answer.

I have seen Dr. Glicksberg put these principles into practice both at New York University, where I was his student, and in the years afterwards, as we have kept in touch. In teaching vocabulary he always gives the derivations of words, both from a linguistic and from a religious point of view, even though it would be more expedient to just have us memorize. Also, aside from his salary as librarian and instructor, I have never known him to accept money for teaching. Over the years he has instructed hundreds of people for free, even when payment was offered. When I needed advice on religious matters, I found that I could call him at home for help. He is also a modest man. Once, in substituting for my regular Hebrew teacher, he gave us the best class we'd had all term. He apologized afterwards, asking us to forgive him if his approach was not what we were used to. The only question I ever asked him to which I did not receive an answer was a philosophical or mystical question (I forget what). He explained that he felt that it was inappropriate to discuss such matters with me at that time. Dr. Glicksberg would never fail a student because he saw no point in doing so. School, he believes, is to educate people, not to sort them.

I read what I have just written and what I wrote in my introduction to the other book and I realize that something is missing. It is hard to convey the intellectual and moral adventure I underwent when I used to study (all of my subjects) in the Jewish Culture Foundation library, tended like a garden by this unusual man. His knowledge of Jewish and linguistic matters seemed encyclopedic, but beyond this I witnessed this unsophisticated man, stubbornly clinging to what he believed in a turbulent, grubby, faddish world. Although the library paid him minimum wage, he still gave a tenth of it to charity. He was not big on publishing, and yet, as best I can judge, he was far more knowledgeable, and a far more capable scholar and better teacher than the tenured professors in the department. He was not stuffy. He made no attempt to force his practices on anyone else, and the same "open house" instruction was available to non-Jews, including non-Jewish clergy, as well as Jews. Yet he was absolutely adamant in his own behavior, no matter how strange that behavior might seem to someone else. When he was ordered to certify teachers who wore short skirts, he simply stopped certifying teachers. I do not share some of his perspectives and beliefs, but I like to think that in some of my better moments I have come to acquire a measure of his stubborness.

Dr. Glicksberg was not treated well in the academic world and never held a tenure-track position. Yet he persisted, because there were people he needed to reach. Now retired, he continues the same work, for free, in his shul and in a neighborhood community center.

When Dr. Glicksberg writes about the Shulchan Aruch, he is not simply writing about what he has studied, but also about what he has lived.

May, 1984	Richard A.G. Friedman
Iyar, 5744	Brooklyn, N.Y.

This book is dedicated to the memory of my late wife, Nechomoh.

INTRODUCTION

The Shulchan Aruch is a codification of Jewish laws which have governed the life of traditional Jews throughout the world from the 16th century to the present day.

The original code was compiled by a Spanish Jew, Joseph Caro, (b. Spain 1488, Safed 1575), whose family was exiled from Spain during the Inquisition, and who, after residing in Turkey, finally settled in Palestine in 1535. An acknowledged scholar, he became the Rosh Yeshivah, i.e., head of the rabbinical Academy of Safed. His crowning achievement was the Shulchan Aruch, which was compiled in Safed, 1542-1554, and published in Venice, 1565.

As a result of the wide dispersion of the Jews and poor communication, Jewish learning at the time of Caro had been reduced to a very low state. Moreover, the new and different local customs with which the Jewish exiles were confronted as they began life in foreign communities created disunity and confusion, adversely affecting their traditional ways. There was urgent need for a unified code expressed in concise language adopted to the educational level of the average Jew. It was to meet this need[1] that Rabbi Caro formulated his compilation. After emendations to the Code were made by Rabbi Moses Isserles, a Polish scholar, (b. Cracow about 1520, d. Cracow 1572), the Shulchan Aruch became the authoritative codification of Jewish law to orthodox Jewry everywhere.

The Problem and the Scope of the Study

This study centered around an examination of the educational principles, practices, and objectives expounded by Joseph Caro in the Shulchan Aruch. Our problem was to determine the particular contributions made by Caro in this Code to Jewish education, and to evaluate them.

We began with the historical, social, and cultural background of Joseph Caro. The biographical data of necessity touched upon some social and educational practices in Turkey and Palestine, where Caro spent most of his life. The aggregate data were presented in the form of a biographical sketch and concluded with a description of the Code, the Shulchan Aruch.

---

1. Joseph Caro. Introduction, *Tur Orach Chayim*, 1882.

An inquiry followed into the nature of the objectives, principles, and practices expounded in the Shulchan Aruch. These were discussed and compared with educational objectives, principles, and practices in modern secular education in the United States.

Subsequently, a study of the sources of Joseph Caro's ideas and practices was made. Thus, the Old Testament, the Mishnah, the Talmud, and several commentaries were cited. Emphasis, however, was placed upon the codes that preceded and that directly influenced Caro's work.

The study then proceeded to compare and analyze the educational objectives, practices, and ideas expounded in the Shulchan Aruch with particular reference to those of theories in Jewish education at later periods. Reference was made to Jewish education in Russia, Poland, the United States, and other countries.

The Need for and Significance of the Study

Preliminary research has shown that there exists no related literature of significance dealing with the educational nature of the Shulchan Aruch, i.e., a critical analysis of its educational principles and practices. The only existing literature directly related to this aspect of our thesis consists of an article, "The Traditional Code of Jewish Education,"[1] by David de Sola Pool, and a book, *The Ethics of the Shulchan Aruch*,[2] by Itzehak Spector. The article contains a short review of the historical background of the Shulchan Aruch followed by excerpts of some of its educational practices. *The Ethics of the Shulchan Aruch*, on the other hand, discusses a selected number of excerpts and examines these in terms of their ethical values, omitting any reference as to their educational relevance.

Considering that the Shulchan Aruch serves as a guide for the observant Jewish layman in his daily behavior and for all phases of his life, this writer has felt the need to examine the educational value of this code.

The significance of our study lies in the value of an analysis of an influential religious code whose educational principles, objectives, and practices have measurably affected life and education among observant Jews.

1. *Cf. Menorah Journal*, June-July, 1924, Vol. 10, Fol. 16, No. 3, p. 270.
2. Itzehak Spector, *The Ethics of the Shulchan Aruch*. Tacoma: Wraith Publishing Company, 1930.

DEFINITION OF TERMS

The following terms which may be found in the body of the thesis are commonly used by Jewish scholars, and may be considered technical terms:

Aggadah (also spelled *Haggadah*) (literally "tale"), the name given to that part of rabbinic literature which contains homiletic exposition of the Bible, stories, legends, folk-lore, anecdotes, or maxims.

Ashkenaz (pl. *Ashkenazim*), a Biblical proper name (Gen. 10:3, I Chron. 1:6, and Jer. 51:27) and a term applied by medieval rabbis to the bulk of northern European Jewry.

Beth-Hamidrash, a portion of the traditional synagogue set aside for study and library purposes.

Caballah (also *Cabbalah*, *Kaballah*), a term applied interchangeably to mystic teachings or laws not explicitly stated in the Old Testament.

Chedar (also *Heder*), a private Hebrew elementary school.

Chumash (also *Humash*), one of the five books of the Pentateuch; often synonymous with the Pentateuch.

Dinim, codified laws, usually referred to those compiled in the Shulchan Aruch.

Gemarah, the original exposition on the Mishnah, known as the Talmud.

Haber ("fellow", "associate"), one scrupulous in the observance of the law; also, a title given formerly to an advanced Talmudic scholar.

Hallachah (also *Hallakah*), a term used for that body of the Talmudic and rabbinic literature which contains legal decisions.

Haskallah, a name applied to the "Enlightenment" movement of the nineteenth-century European Jewry.

Jewish education. For the purpose of this thesis, the term "Jewish Education" is defined as the process of transmission and communication of the Jewish literary heritage, tradition, practices, and mode of life from one generation to another.

Midrash, a term applied to rabbinic literature attempting to interpret and elucidate the non-legal sections of the Bible.

Minhag, a custom.

Mishnah, the bulk of oral laws collected and arranged by Rabbi Judah I ("The Prince"), (b. ca. 135, d. ca. 220) toward the end of the second century. These oral laws form the basis of the Talmudic expositions.

Posekim (literally "codifiers"), a term given to the bulk of codified rabbinic literature, it includes Joseph Caro's *Beth Yosef* and the *Shulchan Aruch*.

Rabbi, one ordained to pass on Jewish Law.

Rosh Yeshivah, the head of a rabbinical academy.

Sanhedrin (also referred to as *Synhedrion*), a body of learned men in whom was vested the authority to decide questions of Jewish law. It was abolished by Rome in 70 C.E.

Semichah, confermant of the title of rabbi (referring to various Biblical injunctions, e.g., Ex. 29:10,19).

Sephardi (pl. *Sephardim*), reference to Obadia, Verse 20, a term applied by Jewish literature of the Middle Ages to the bulk of South European Jewry.

Shulchan Aruch (literally "A prepared table"), the name of the authoritative Jewish Code of law (reference to Ex. 23:41).

Talmud, the body of Jewish law and traditions, including the *Mishnah* (see *Mishnah*), compiled by Rab Ashi, a Babylonian scholar (b. 352, d. 427); its first compilation was about 500 C.E.

Talmud Torah, an elementary Hebrew school supported by private citizens.

Torah, refers interchangeably to the Old Testament, the Talmud, and rabbinic literature.

Yeshivah, a rabbinic college.

CHAPTER I

JOSEPH CARO AND THE BACKGROUND OF THE SHULCHAN ARUCH

The Shulchan Aruch[1]

The Shulchan Aruch, ("prepared table" in Hebrew), is the standard digest of Jewish practice. It sums up the organized development of three thousand years of Jewish life.[2] The Shulchan Aruch is based on the Bible, the Mishnah,[3] the Talmud,[4] and on post-Talmudic literature such as responsa and rulings rendered by various rabbis; on laws and customs developed in several countries and embodied in isolated decisions and in special collections of rulings; on local precedents; on standards set up by individual rabbis and rabbinical colleges;[5] and on commentaries on the Talmud.

Different authors have at various times written their own versions of the Shulchan Aruch. For instance, Mordechai Jaffe, 1530-1612, wrote the *Lebushim*, a somewhat more discursive and explicit version of the Shulchan Aruch; Isaac Ben Shelomo Ashkenazi, known as the ARI, 1534-1572, wrote *The Shulchan Aruch shel ARI*, a mystical explanation of the laws expounded in the Shulchan Aruch; Shelomo Ganzfried, 1800-1848, wrote the *Kitzur Shulchan Aruch*, selecting only such laws as he deemed absolutely necessary; and Abraham ben Jehiel Danzig, ca. 1747-1820, wrote the *Hayye Adam* and the *Hokmat Adam* in which he added decisions that had been accepted during the two hundred and fifty years after Caro, an interpretation tending toward the ethical.

In the course of time this material had become so voluminous and unwieldy that rabbis had considerable difficulty finding the legal decisions they sought for application to current cases. Several codes were written prior to the Shulchan Aruch, but none was fully accepted.

It remained for Joseph Caro,[6] an illustrious rabbi of the sixteenth century whose family had been expelled from Spain,[7] to produce a code of Jewish law acceptable to the mass of Jewry.

Caro decided to write an extensive commentary that would include not only the sources of each decision but also a critical analysis of the sources and the opinions of scholars that had been omitted[8] from the various codes. He

1

appended his commentary to the *Arba Turim*, an earlier code by Jacob ben Asher (1280–1340) "because it includes the majority of the decisions of the rabbis,"[9] and followed this code's arrangement of four divisions. This commentary is the *Beth Yoseph*.

Since the *Beth Yoseph* is the basis of the Shulchan Aruch, the circumstances of its composition and of its impact upon world Jewry deserve further consideration. The addition of the sources made the code an authoritative text; the prestige it attained made it the foremost religious code.

We have already noted that the sheer accumulation of decisions, rulings, and commentaries had formed an unwieldy mass, almost unusable as a guide to the rabbis who were responsible for maintaining order and preserving tradition in the Jewish communities. The rabbis of Caro's day had to cope not only with the inaccessibility of past decisions and rulings in the Talmud, but also with a multitude of relatively recent, conflicting decisions disseminated through the medium of printing.[10] And as we have also noted, earlier efforts to reduce the chaos had been unsatisfactory. The dispersion and wanderings of the Jews made learning difficult. Caro's aim in the *Beth Yoseph* was to give unity to the interpretations of the Bible, and to compile a well organized code, so that "if someone has it in front of him he will find the contents of the Talmud arranged systematically."[11] In the words of Graetz, "It was this confusion and divergence of opinion that Joseph Karo wished to check by means of his new religious code."[12] Yaavetz[13] felt that Caro's work laid the basis for unity among the Jews throughout the dispersion.

In 1550, when the *Beth Yoseph* appeared, the impact was tremendous. Caro was immediately recognized as one of the greatest Talmudic scholars, and his code soon superseded all previous ones. It was promptly accepted by two hundred rabbis as the standard code, and its fame reached even remote Jewish communities.[14] Scholars felt that Caro was the "only rabbi who left to posterity an epoch-making work, disputed though it be."[15] In its original form the *Beth Yoseph* was appreciated only by the scholar, for "even to understand the *Beth Yoseph* implied . . . profound scholarship."[16] The *Beth Yoseph* is better known to the Orthodox Jewish laymen in its abridged form as the Shulchan Aruch. Actually it is used in an abridged form known as the *Kitzur*, i.e., abbreviation.

The laws codified by Caro in his *Beth Yoseph* were based chiefly on Sephardic authorities and customs prevalent among Sephardic Jews. The contention was that he deliberately disregarded decisions and customs of the Ashkenazic Jews.[17] This basis of selection was reflected in the Shulchan Aruch. Although the controversial issues in the *Beth Yoseph* were discussed by Jewish scholars and rabbis, both Sephardic and Ashkenazic, Caro's partiality towards the Sephardic interpretation in the Shulchan Aruch tended to limit its acceptance for the first twenty years to the Spanish communities.[18] For the Ashkenazic Jews, who "were much more scrupulous in matters of ritual than their Spanish-Portuguese brethren,[19] Caro's rulings were regarded as too lax in some instances.

The first edition of Caro's Shulchan Aruch appeared in Venice in 1565. The need for a simplified code for the Ashkenazic communities was acute enough to move Rabbi Moses Isserles (1530–1572), a Polish scholar, to amend the Shulchan Aruch, bringing it into accord with Ashkenazic usage. Because of the prestige Isserles enjoyed, the code with his emendations became the final authority among the Ashkenazic Jews.[20] After Isserles had made the necessary changes, the editors in Poland automatically inserted them alongside the decisions included by Caro.[21] We should note, however, that the emendations of Rabbi Moses Isserles added weight to Caro's authority.[22]

In writing the *Beth Yoseph*, Caro sought to raise the general level of Jewish learning, to give unity to interpretations of the Bible, and by means of a well-organized code to provide guidance for the decisions of the rabbis. In writing the Shulchan Aruch, he was concerned specifically with teaching the law to the laity,[23] so inculcating it "that they would know it by heart . . . and the young students would be acquainted with it from their earliest age, practice its precepts, and would not turn from it even when they grow old."[24] To accomplish his aim, Caro had his code printed in the form of a textbook with the contents divided into thirty lessons to be covered at the rate of one lesson a day for one month. The study was to be repeated each month.[25] According to Waxman, "Karo also introduced the division of chapters into paragraphs, the number of paragraphs varying according to the contents of each chapter."[26]

The importance of the Shulchan Aruch to the Jews at that time cannot be overestimated. It came when many Jews lived in uncertainty and were suffering persecution and expulsion—circumstances that disrupted study and meditation.[27] The fact that the code was prepared for the average Jew and the "young student" added to its importance and hastened its acceptance. The code soon became the infallible authority throughout the diaspora.[28] Translations were made for those who did not understand Hebrew.[29]

General acceptance of the Shulchan Aruch did not preclude opposition to it. Some rabbis opposed the code on the ground that it would suppress local variations.[30] Others felt that the Talmud alone should be the final authority in rendering decisions,[31] even at the cost of disagreement and contradiction. Still others thought the code was outmoded and not suitable for Jews living in the countries where customs and practices ran counter to those codified in the Shulchan Aruch, as for instance with regard to laws that sanction intermarriage.[32]

However, despite controversy on many points which sprang up almost from the moment Joseph Caro first published the Shulchan Aruch, and which has continued to this day, the unifying effect of this work for world Jewry should not be underestimated.[33] The life and times of the author of the Shulchan Aruch are without doubt reflected in this codification of the laws, and bear examination.

Joseph Caro

Joseph Caro and his father were among those who migrated to Turkey at the beginning of the sixteenth century as a result of the expulsion of the Jews from Spain. With the exception of his first eight years in Spain and Portugal, Joseph Caro spent his life in Turkey and Palestine. His education and outlook were naturally shaped by both the customs and traditions of his co-religionists, and by the native cultures of these countries.

Joseph Caro lived and worked amidst the diverse and sometimes conflicting currents of life in Jewish communities, more or less influenced by their secular environments. He "was considered by the scholars of the day as the greatest man in his generation"[34] who "decided what was Judaism."[35] Caro encountered three distinct cultures: the Spanish-Portuguese Jewish culture in early childhood, and the Palestinian-Jewish culture in the period of his maturity. A more detailed examination of his life and career will describe the secular and religious forces that molded Caro, and will delineate the influence he in turn exerted on his fellow Jews.

Because of the comparatively scarce biographical material available on Caro,[36] scholars are uncertain about the exact date of his birth, his itinerary, and who his teachers were.[37]

Joseph Caro, born in Toledo, Spain in 1488[38] was a descendant of a highly gifted and esteemed family.[39] His father, Ephraim, was an eminent rabbi and Talmudist. In 1492, when the Jews were expelled from Spain, Joseph was four years old. His parents took him to Portugal[40] where his paternal uncle, Isaac Caro, head of a rabbinical academy, resided. Later, in 1496, the expulsion of the Jews from Portugal drove the Caro family to Turkey.[41]

There are no definite data on Caro's childhood education, and the conjectures of scholars vary. Among these conjectures are the following:

> When four years old, while in Nicopolis, he (Joseph Caro) learned directly from his father.[42]
>
> The wandering periods were for young Caro the periods of study.[43]
>
> Caro was educated by his father and other Spanish rabbis.[44]
>
> In Portugal Caro received his first instruction from his father and also became the pupil of his (Joseph Caro's) friend and teacher, Jacob Berab.[45]
>
> Caro's uncle, Isaac, probably instructed Joseph upon his arrival in Turkey.[46]

> Joseph Caro was born in the Pyrenean peninsula (probably Spain) in the year 1488, whence he emigrated as a boy of four, in the year 1492, with his father Ephraim, who was his first teacher.[47]
>
> Joseph Caro, our Master, was born in Toledo, Spain, in the year 1488. He was the son of Rabbi Ephraim, the Rabbi of Nicopolis, and of Mrs. Busne. His first instruction he received from his father... In Lisbon [Portugal], he was the student of Berab.... Later he became the student of his uncle, Itzhak Caro.[48]

The most reliable summary seems to be that Caro probably began his education at the age of three,[49] while still in Toledo.[50] When he arrived at Lisbon, in all likelihood, he redoubled his efforts to make up for time lost, studying under the guidance and supervision of his father,[51] his uncle, and his friend, Jacob Berab.[52] His official schooling seems to have begun at the age of four or five. The subject matter studied by the children of devout families was the Pentateuch and the Mishnah. This phase of his education probably continued until about the end of 1496, when he was about eight years old. By that time he may already have been well versed in the contents of the Pentateuch and in a considerable part of the Mishnah, and he had perhaps even been introduced to some small tractates of the Talmud.[53] With this probable educational background, Caro left Portugal for Turkey.

Caro arrived in Turkey sometime between 1496 and 1498.[54] His father settled in Nicopolis[55] and a short time afterwards was elected to the office of chief rabbi, the former incumbent having recently died. Joseph pursued his studies intensively under the guidance of both his father and his uncle. When he reached "the age of about ten or eleven he was already famous as a scholar in the Talmud and *halachah*."[56]

In Nicopolis, Caro married the daughter of the late rabbi, but she died "without issue"[57] soon after he had been elected chief rabbi, on his father's death. While he was in Nicopolis, Caro wrote a commentary on Maimonides' *Yad Hachazakah* entitled *Keseph Mishneh*.[58]

In 1516 Caro's uncle left for Palestine,[59] and in 1520, Caro left Nicopolis and settled in Adrianople where he was invited to head a rabbinical academy.[60] Although occupied with his duties at the academy, he nevertheless began to compose his famous commentary, *Beth Yoseph*, which later became the basis for the even more famous Shulchan Aruch.[61] Research on this commentary required him to make "several journeys to Constantinople and Salonica in search of material."[62] During his fourteen-year residence in Adrianople, he married for the second time.[63]

Caro left for Safed, Palestine, about 1534, arriving in 1536. Most writers ascribe his decision to go to Safed, the center of Jewish mysticism, to the belief prevalent among the Jews that the Messiah was about to arrive.[64] Mystical calculations fixed the year 1540 for the event.[65] Some writers even maintain that the belief in the coming of the Messiah stimulated Caro to write his *Beth Yoseph*.[66]

Jacob Berab (1474–1546), Caro's one-time teacher and his friend, was chief rabbi in Safed. He was particularly active in the movement "to create a spiritual center for the Jews scattered throughout the world by reestablishing ordination,"[67] which he considered one of the prerequisites to the coming of the Messiah. Berab had himself been ordained by other rabbis, and in turn ordained Caro among others, "as a member of the synhedrion."[68] After the death of Jacob Berab on April 4, 1546, Caro was elected chief rabbi of Safed.[69] He tried to continue the newly reinstated ordination, but because of strong opposition on the part of eminent rabbis, he gave up the attempt.

With the assistance of Jacob Berab, Caro completed his *Beth Yoseph*[70] in 1542. He spent the next twelve years revising it, and then compiled the simplified and abridged version which we know as the Shulchan Aruch. When he noticed that the *Beth Yoseph* contained some obscure passages, he wrote a special commentary on them, the *Bedek Habbayit* (The Repair of the House).[71]

In 1555, Caro's second wife bore him a son, Solomon.[72] Some time between 1555 and 1565, she died,[73] and in 1565 Caro married for the third time. His third wife also gave birth to a son, Judah, in 1571.[74] Caro was eighty-three at that time. In his eighty-seventh year (1575), Caro fell victim to an epidemic and died. His death caused deep mourning among the Jews the world over.[75]

Caro was not merely a scholar in Talmudic and rabbinic literature. His writings reveal an intellectual honesty attracting the reader by his use of plain, easily understood words, appealing to the heart as well as the mind. Caro was candid in admitting his own limitations. He made no pretense about possessing a perfect memory of the Talmudic references. For example, Maimonides, in his tractate on the acquisition of good characteristics, suggests that one should avoid unnecessary speech, using it only to express words of widsom or such words as are absolutely necessary. To cite an authority for his advice, Maimonides remarks that Rav, the disciple of Rabenu, never uttered an unnecessary word.[76] Regarding this statement, Caro remarks in his commentary, the *Kesef Mishneh*, "I found such statement about R. Yokhanan b. Zakkai,[77] but on Rav, I do not know at the moment the place." This quality of honesty permeates the Shulchan Aruch.

The Jewish Community in Turkey in Caro's Time

The Jewish community in Turkey in the sixteenth century represented a conglomeration of Jews who had come from various parts of the world to seek refuge there.[78] It was the era which witnessed the expulsion from Spain and Portugal and the consequent tragic decline of Jewish life in these countries; it was the era which also ushered in great prosperity, material and spiritual, for the Jews who had fled from those countries and who had taken up the challenge of life in Turkey. This was the period of the Ottoman Empire's expansion under liberal Sultans. According to Goodblatt,[79]

> The sultans of Turkey were committed to a policy, decreed by their religion, to conquer unbelievers who must be converted to Islam, subjected to tribute or destroyed by the sword. Yet the administration of justice and the treatment of non-Moslems were more liberal than in Christian countries. These were influenced by the moral teachings of Islam that nothing is of higher importance than justice and the protection of the oppressed.... Christians and Jews were, as a matter of policy, permitted to exercise their religion during the rule of Sulaimon, at the very time when the Inquisition was carrying on its deadly work in Spain.

The liberal Sultans[80] were especially appreciative of the professional knowledge and manual skills the Jews had brought with them from Spain and elsewhere.[81] Some Jews actively participated in the various branches of government and in social life.

It is therefore possible that the educational program for the Jews, formal and informal, which Caro formulated in the Shulchan Aruch, is influenced by his experiences in these countries. A discussion of education in Turkey and Palestine at that time[82] will also contribute to a better understanding of Caro's educational plan.

Jewish Education in Turkey

Elementary Education

Elementary Jewish education in Turkey early in the sixteenth century, when Joseph Caro lived there (ca. 1496-ca. 1534) followed the general lines of that in the extant Jewish communities everywhere.[83] Because of the differences in the social and cultural backgrounds of the Jews in Turkey, "no fixed pattern prevailed,"[84] but religious education and character training formed a common base. Even infants were taught to observe some rituals and to say benedictions, and they were taken to synagogue services.[85]

Goodblatt states that the Jewish community in Turkey supported two elementary schools, public and private. While he does not report the curriculum content, we may assume that it followed by and large the general trend of Jewish education in Europe.

If a boy had not learned to read at home by the age of about five,[86] he was sent to the elementary school and there taught to recognize and subsequently to read the Hebrew alphabet. He then proceeded to the study of the Pentateuch, beginning with the book of Leviticus.[87] Next he was taught the weekly portion of the Pentateuch[88] in Hebrew, which he later learned in the Arabic vernacular. At about the age of seven, the average boy was introduced to the books of the Prophets and to the Hagiographa, the historical portion of the Old Testament. When he reached ten, the boy began to study the Mishnah; and by the time he reached the age of thirteen, he had read a selection of the most important small tractates of the Talmud. Boys usually spent about seven years in elementary school.[89]

Adult Education

Although elementary education followed more or less the same pattern among both the Sephardim and the Ashkenazim, the curricula usually diverged thereafter. The Sephardic Jews tended to include secular subjects along with the usual religious studies in the education of their young men. This was also the practice of Turkish Jews before 1492,[90] the year when mass migration of European Jews into Turkey began. After the Sephardic youth had completed the stipulated program of religious education, he moved on to secular subjects which were, however, considered only as supplementary to religion.[91] These subjects included philosophy, mathematics, geometry, astronomy, medicine, poetry, grammar, and music.

Simcha Asaf,[92] quoting from Moses ben Baruch Almosnino's (Salonica 1510–Constantinople ca. 1580) work, *Regimiento de la Vida*,[93] brings us another example of a curriculum intended to supplement the religious education of youngsters. Eager to save precious time, and "because life is so short and work aplenty," Almosnino suggested the following basic selection that would be helpful to the understanding of the Talmud, namely, logic, arithmetic, geography and astrology. The other subjects, such as grammar, rhetoric, geometry, music, perspective (drawing?) were not deemed necessary for the student of the Talmud. Thus we note that the curriculum of the Jewish youth in Turkey included both religious and some secular subjects, the latter as aids to the religious studies.

Asaf informs us also,[94] quoting Moses ben Hagiz (1660–1751) from his work *Mishnath Chachamim*,[95] that his father, Yacob Hagiz, suggested the correct way to educate a child was by first teaching him the Bible, including the Prophets and Hagiographa, then concentrating on Gemara until he reaches the age of twenty. This, he said, was done in Poland, Germany, most of Turkey, and Italy, and the custom was also instituted in Jerusalem, Upper Galilee, and Safed during the time of the famous Joseph Caro.

The education of the Jews of Central European countries was confined to religious matters "based exclusively on the Talmud."[96] The Ashkenazic youth might continue his Talmudic education even after marriage, "and to the end of his life the earning of his livelihood was held to be of secondary importance."[97] Not infrequently the husband would devote his entire life only to the study of the law while his wife would willingly support the family.[98] Among the Ashkenazim, the study of secular matters was limited to the material found in rabbinical literature and was used only to clarify Biblical passage.[99]

Education of Jewish Women

At the beginning of the sixteenth century, there was no formal program of education for Jewish women. They did, however, receive instruction in the Bible and in such secular subjects as "grammar, arithmetic, geography and history . . . necessary for a better understanding of the Scriptures."[100] Further, the observing of ritualistic prescriptions gave them "considerable knowledge of Biblical and rabbinical law."[101]

We are informed by Simcha Asaf,[102] quoting Rabbi Itzchak ben R. Abraham Molcho, from his work *Orchoth Yosher*,[103] that it is better that the teacher for women should teach them the blessings in the vernacular rather than teach them Aggadah.

Since in Turkey "the Jewish minority was granted full autonomy to worship, open schools, and follow its cultural activities,"[104] it may be assumed that the Jewish congregations availed themselves of the opportunity to give their young women at least the religious education necessary to prepare them for their duties as housewives, and the secular education necessary to maintain their social standing.

General Education in Turkey

Turkish education had reached a high standard by the beginning of the sixteenth century. Elementary schools "were established in all the Islamic countries."[105] These schools provided education for both boys and girls who began to attend school at the age of five. The curriculum consisted of reading, writing, religion, grammar, versification, arithmetic, and geography.[106] The secondary public school system, also widespread, in Turkey, offered a curriculum consisting of grammar, logic, metaphysics, philology, military science, rhetoric, geometry, and astronomy.[107]

Besides the elementary and secondary public school systems, the sultans provided special educational opportunities for military and court functionaries at the Palace School.[108] There the curricula were designed "to produce . . . the warrior-statesman and loyal Moslem—'a man of letters and a gentleman of polished speech, profound courtesy, and honest morals.' "[109] In the main, however, the subjects of study were adapted to the intellectual capacities and manual skills of the students as well as to the needs of the government.[110]

We have a less inspiring picture of the education of Turkish women. Although girls attended the elementary schools, it seems they did not continue their education beyond that. Moslem tradition accorded women a passive and minor role in the decisions of daily life. "Generally the Turkish women lived within their compounds of their houses, girls grew up behind their latticed windows, and their husbands were chosen by their parents."[111] Husbands could divorce their wives without recourse to legal procedure.[112]

The Jewish Community in Palestine in Caro's Time

Palestine was under Turkish rule in the sixteenth century. To the Jews of Turkey, it was the "Holy Land," the spiritual center, recognized as such because of its tradition of ancient glory.[113] And so it has remained to this day, with very few exceptions, to Jews the world over.

Even after the exile, Jews would meet in groups in Palestine during festivals. But these meetings were brought to a standstill in the eleventh century, because of the troubles caused by the Crusades. During the second decade of the thirteenth century[114] Jews renewed their pilgrimages to Palestine, culminating with three hundred rabbis from Europe, England, and Spain. Thereafter, Jews would come and settle in vairous parts of the country.

Jewish immigration into Palestine increased markedly after 1492, following the Inquisition in Spain and persecution in other countries.[115] Many of the immigrants and refugees were of high social and intellectual status and settled in Safed, a small city in Upper Galilee, thus making it a center of learning in Palestine.[116] Schechter points out that the history of the sixteenth-century Safed is largely that of the two outstanding personalities of the time, namely "R. Joseph Caro, the leading light of the time, and his contemporary, R. Isaac Luria (Jerusalem 1534–d. Safed 1572), the generally recognized head of the mystical school of Safed."[117]

Shlomel of Moravia, writing in 1603, states in a letter that Safed contained eighteen Talmudic colleges and twenty-one synagogues, a large school for the children of the poor with twenty teachers and nearly four hundred pupils. He also states that among the people of Safed, there were "great scholars, saints, and men of action, full of Divine wisdom, so that they were worthy of the gift of the Holy Spirit."[118]

The people of Safed earned their livelihood in various ways. The natives engaged in peddling or cultivating the ground in the neighboring villages. The immigrants engaged in trading "exporting grain, wine, and oil . . . and importing from the articles for which there was a demand in Safed. There also grew up in Safed a large trade in the weaving of wool and in the manufacturing of clothes."[119]

Jewish Education in Palestine during the Sixteenth Century

We have noted that the Jewish population in Palestine increased after 1492. We have also noted that Safed became the center of learning in Palestine. We will now describe the status of Jewish education in Palestine, particularly during the time when Joseph Caro lived and worked there.

After centuries of slumber, Jewish education revived in the sixteenth century. The curriculum followed in Palestinian schools at the time had been a symbol and an example for many communities in the Diaspora. Asaf,[120] for instance, informs us that the status of Jewish education in the land of Israel during the sixteenth and the seventeenth centuries, especially in Safed, was on a higher level than that in Poland, Lithuania, and Germany of the new period. He further states that leading educators in various countries looked up to the teaching curricula in Palestine.[121]

It is interesting to note that Israel Elfenbein, in his essay on "Jewish Education in Palestine under Turkey,"[122] found it necessary, almost at the beginning of the essay, to write about the moral standards of the teacher. He describes the teacher as one who "possessed the qualifications for integrity, piety, and efficiency."[123] He also points out that the teacher enjoyed the privilege of tax exemption,[124] which may be interpreted to mean that the teacher's status was important to the community, that he was viewed as one who helps shape the future of the community.

The active instruction of the child began at home,[125] as soon as the child began to speak. It was the custom to bring the child to school at the early age of two or three in order to train him in the Hebrew alphabet and vowels. There were, however, parents who did not bring their children to school until they were five.[126]

Between the ages of six and seven, the child was taught the Pentateuch, the Prophets, Jewish history, and Hebrew grammar.[127] From the age of seven until his thirteenth year, when the child became *bar-mitzvah*, he was taught the following subjects: "Bible with the commentary of Rashi (1040-1105), Midrash or Exegesis, Aggadah and the Laws"[129] which were needed for his guidance in problems of religious, social and private life. At the age of ten the youth was taught Mishnah with the commentary of Obadiah Bertinoro (b. Italy?- d. Jerusalem ca. 1500), and the Gemara with the commentary of Rashi, twice or three times weekly.[130] By the time he reached the thirteenth year, he had finished the six Orders of the Mishnah. In Galilee the curriculum required the boy to study during one year, the following three Orders of the Mishnah: Moed (dealing with the laws concerning Sabbath, festivals, and days of fast), Nezikin (dealing with criminal and civic jurisprudence), and Nashim (dealing with marriage, divorce, and the position of women in Judaism; and only eight months were allotted to each of the remaining three Orders, namely Kodashim (dealing with sacrifices), Tohoroth (dealing with cleanliness), and Zerayim (dealing primarily with agricultural laws).[131] This, then, was the curriculum for the average young Jew, if he was to embark upon a career of a merchant or craftsman. These subjects were deemed indispensable to one "who bears the name of an Israelite.[132]

If the father decided that his son embark upon the career of a Master of Law or Rabbi, then the young man continued to study the Gemara and cognate Talmudical subjects until the age of twenty.[133]

In some Talmudical colleges the curriculum varied. Thus, Rabbi Moses

Alshech, describing the curriculum of a Talmudical college in Safed,[134] says that the nights were spent in research, while the days were spent in the study of the Law with afternoons devoted to study of the Posekim or Codes. Fridays were set aside for reading the Scriptures and the Midrash or Exegesis, dealing with the current portion of the week.

Changes in curriculum are also noted from a letter written by the "sons of the Yeshivah"[135] in Jerusalem, dated 1521. The study contains the Talmud with Rashi and the French Tosafists (commentators) of which in the morning they cover, as a rule, one or two folios.[136] In the evening they would finish one chapter of both the Mishnah and the Code of Maimonides.[137]

The sages prescribed for the various stages of Jewish studies are those specified in the Mishnah (Aboth V:20), namely, "Five years [is the age] for [the study of] Scriptures, ten for [the study of] Mishnah, thirteen for [becoming subject to] commandents, fifteen for [the study of] Talmud . . ."[138]

Education of Women

There seems to have been no specific provision for the education of Jewish women in Palestine in the sixteenth century. We are informed,[139] however, that "In Upper Galilee, including Safed, we find private teachers who taught the prayers and blessings to the women and beginners."[140] Schechter[141] also reports about special teachers "to instruct women and children in the liturgy and in the prescribed benedictions."[142]

The education of women appears, then, to have been limited to those biblical precepts designed to prepare them for the task of promoting the moral and social well-being of the home and the community.

Adult Education

Asaf,[143] quoting Zechariah ben Saadiah, who visited Safed in 1561, notes that many people came to listen to the lectures offered in the synagogues. He also quotes Shlumel[144] who says that soon after the morning and evening services, the worshippers in the synagogues organized themselves into a number of study groups. One group studied the Code of Maimonides regularly, another the Ein Yaacov, a third a Talmudic tractate, a fourth the Mishnah, and still another group the Hallachah with the commentaries of Rashi and the Tosafists. . . . Others were engated in the study of the Zohar, the Torah, the Prophets, and Hagiographa. There was hardly a single worshipper who did not devote time to study before leaving for the day's work. The same was true at night, before the people departed for their homes.[145]

Elfenbein[146] points out that in Jerusalem, the Jews who were not engaged in work or commerce, would remain in the synagogue to listen to the Darshan or preacher for fifteen minutes, and would then proceed to the Bet HaMidrash "where they studied Mishnah and Gemara for a period of six hours."

The Curriculum of the Schools of the Mystics

In Joseph Caro's time, the adherents of mysticism believed that the Messiah would appear in the near future. This movement influenced education, especially in Safed where the mystic movement predominated, and where it "gained directness and popularity (shaping) new attitudes and social customs."[147]

The Talmud and its allied literature continued to be the subjects of study among the non-mystics; the mystics, however, "Had become so entirely absorbed in the Cabbalistic teachings... that the study of the Talmud was greatly neglected."[148]

Rabbi Moses Cordovero (1522-1570), head of a school of mystics, pointed out a curriculum for study to be pursued by the members of his school.[149] This curriculum consisted in part of specific rules of behavior; however, we will discuss the curriculum in terms of subject matter:

We note Rule Number 33. *Haber* (a title of honor given to an advanced Talmudic scholar) "should busy himself every day with the study of the Bible, the Mishnah, Talmud, Cabbala, and Law." Under Rule Number 36, we find a number of sub-rules. One of them requires the Haber to study the Mishnah every Friday night "as much as he can." Another sub-rule requires the Haber to review the Mishnah each week. And a third sub-rule requires him to learn by heart at least two sections of the Mishnah each week.[150]

From a list of rules by Abraham Galanti, the leading disciple of the above-mentioned Moses Cordovero, we note that he urges his disciples (Rule 21) to set aside fixed time by day and night for the study of Torah.[151]

It would appear that the rules for some of the schools of the mystics were at variance with those of others, since in some the study of Cabbala was stressed above all other teachings, while in others (such as Rabbi Cordovero's), Cabbala was studied in conjunction with the Bible, the Mishnah, the Talmud, and the Law.

CHAPTER II

THE BASIC EDUCATIONAL PRINCIPLES AND PRACTICES IN THE SHULCHAN ARUCH

This chapter is concerned with a discussion of the educational principles and practices of Jewish education expounded in the Shulchan Aruch. We shall accordingly proceed to examine the educational implications of the Code as they relate to the harmonious development of the individual in relation to society.

Physical Development

Rest

In a curriculum intended to develop men whose chief occupation would be to serve God and to study the Law, one cannot expect a formal program of physical education. Nevertheless, physical education based on the principles of good health and personal hygiene, healthful food habits, and recreational activity, while not included in a formal curriculum,[1] are provided for informally.

Physical rest is essential to good health. The Shulchan Aruch provides for the observance of the Sabbath as a day of spiritual rest and physical relaxation and proscribes numerous activities for that day and other holy days. The rules calling for the rigid observance of the Sabbath and festivals express by implication a concern for physical well-being.

Health and Hygiene

In the Shulchan Aruch, most of the educational principles relating to health and hygiene are also to be inferred from laws intended primarily to regulate ritual practice, but bearing educational implications.

The curing of illness is enjoined on physician and patient alike. (The physician is ordered by the Torah to cure illness and strive to save life; anyone who neglects his own illness is compared to a murderer.)[2]

Caring for the sick is permitted even if it means breaking holy-day laws. Relating to the Sabbath:

Every [case of] lifesaving defers the laws of the Sabbath, and one who is alert to save a life is praiseworthy.[3]

One may extinguish a candle on the Sabbath to enable a sick person to sleep.[4]

Ritual slaughtering and cooking for the sick are permitted on the Sabbath.[5]

It is permissible on the Sabbath to wash and remove pus from one's eyes. If, on the ninth of Ab,[6] there is pus in one's eyes . . . one should wash them and remove the pus without hesitation.[7]

Even the strictures for the Day of Atonement are flexible. Thus, even if a person is ill but not dangerously so, a person's body may be anointed on the sacred day, an act normally forbidden.[8] If fasting causes faintness, as indicated by diminishing eyesight, one may be fed until normal vision returns. Indeed, even forbidden food may be eaten if permissible substance is unavailable.[9]

Consideration is given to the physical needs of children and to special conditions. To avoid danger to health, children under nine should not be compelled to fast on the Day of Atonement.[10] Where the climate is cold, a fire may be kindled on the Sabbath for children to warm themselves. Even adults may draw near the fire on very cold days.[11]

The principle that cleanliness is essential to good health[12] underlies education in hygiene. Stress is laid on the frequent washing of the hands.[13] Upon arising, upon leaving the toilet or bath, after cutting one's nails, removing one's shoes, touching one's feet, rubbing one's head, coming in contact with insects; and other instances involving contamination and uncleanliness.[14] Before washing one's hands,[15] it is strictly forbidden to touch the mouth, nose, ears, or eyes.

To encourage prevention of communicable diseases, rules were promulgated forbidding the offering of drink to another in a cup from which one has drunk previously,[16] or the drinking of water which has become discolored, possibly because of pollution.[17]

Food

The subject of food is discussed in the Shulchan Aruch chiefly from the point of views of religion or aesthetics;[18] the nutritional value of food is not considered.[19] But healthful food habits are prescribed and the underlying principles explained in terms of maintaining a healthy body able to serve God. Thus, it is urged that breakfast be eaten no later than four hours after sunrise. Even the scholar is cautioned not to abstain from food longer than six hours after sunrise:

> for if he has not eaten something in the early morning hours, it [eating food] is [like] throwing a stone into a skin bottle.[20]

One may eat lightly before the entire service has been completed (before the Musaf services)[21] in order to refresh oneself.[22] And it is advised to eat moderately easily digested food on the eve of the Day of Atonement,[23] before beginning the fast.

The Shulchan Aruch also provides us with incidental information concerning the value of salt and water with meals:

> If one has eaten a meal without salt [and if] he has not drunk water, [then] during the day he should worry about mouth odor and at night about [both] mouth odor and choking.[24]

Recreation

Physical activities such as sports, games, and spontaneous play are referred to in the Shulchan Aruch as informal recreational activity. This informality permits the operation of the first two principles of physical education. According to Curoe: "The *first* educational principle . . . is that a child cannot be forced to play . . . the *second* principle is that physical activities are not play unless they are pleasurable."[25]

In the Code, references to recreational activity invariably carry some religious implications. As in the case of provisions for health and hygiene, we learn about these activities indirectly, again, usually from the laws governing the Sabbath and other holy days. Boys are permitted to enjoy games on the Sabbath[26] but ball playing is forbidden,[27] either because the ball might, while in motion, indent an earthen floor (which is considered work), or because the object might move from a public to a private place, which is also foribdden.[28] And because gymnastic activities cause overwork and perspiration, these too are forbidden on the Sabbath.[29]

Many recreational activities are forbidden lest they lead to acts forbidden on the Sabbath. Thus games requiring the use of nuts or similar objects are proscribed because these too could lead to making indentations on the floor.[30] Swimming in the pool of one's back yard, however, is permitted[31] if the pool has a rim around it to keep water from overflowing. However, "one should not beat palm on palm and dance," because that may eventually lead to the tuning of instruments and to the possibility of repairing broken strings, which, of course, is prohibited as involving labor on the Sabbath.[32]

The importance of the Sabbath as a day of rest, which is inherently an important health measure, is indicated by the ordinance that a person is forbidden to ring chimes even for the children's entertainment. However, if prepared in advance, "a bell that rings by itself by means of a contraption set up the day before,"[33] is permissible since no labor is required for such an amusement on the part of anyone.

The rules governing recreational activities during some holy days are not so strict as in the Sabbath laws. Thus we note that "whoever wishes to enjoy horseback riding on the intermediate[34] days may shoe the horses and work on the saddle, bridle, and all riding implements."[35]

Writing, which is labor or an approximation of labor, must also have been included among recreational activities, for we read:

> One should be careful not to write with his finger in water [spilled] upon the table or on soil, but it is permissible to draw letter-like figures in the air.[36]

The Shulchan Aruch prohibits a recreational activity that would produce a terrorizing effect such as to leave impressions of fear or terror on children. For example, the wearing of a mask to frighten children was proscribed.[37]

Moral and Ethical Development

Education in the Code is primarily religious and moral. Its goals are the study of the Torah as a guide, obedience to its teachings, and the development of character.[38] To achieve these ends, the Code implies specific educational principles such as arousing interest and stimulating effort, learning by doing, recognizing individual differences, training of memory, inculcating right attitudes and habits, and correlating learning.

Arousing Interest and Stimulating Effort

The psychological principles of getting attention reduce themselves to two, *viz.*, to arouse interest and to secure effort.[39]

The Code attempts to arouse interest and stimulate effort for the development of character traits and proper behavior, especially in the study of the Torah.[40]

In Jewish life, the study of the Torah is considered the chief means of serving God, and to such study are attached the highest social and spiritual values. The Code emphasizes these values.[41] For many Jewish students, therefore, study of the Torah constitutes an immediate interest, one in which according to Klapper, the desire and the end are one.[42] Learning to read is a mediate interest, the kind of interest that is aroused when "we must go through an uninteresting process in order to attain a desired end . . . The child who learns his letters . . . to be able to read the interesting stories that the teacher tells the class is actuated by a mediate interest."[43] In orthodox Jewish education the chief end desired is the ability to read the holy books.

By emphasizing the value of studying the Torah and stating the means of achieving this end, the Code seeks to encourage the studious, and to stimulate effort in those whose attention might have wandered from the things of God to the things of the world. Moreover, the nights are not to be spent in eating, drinking, idle talk, or too much sleep, but "only in the words of wisdom and [in] the study of the Torah."[44]

Special exhortations are found urging that a good part of the night be used for study, "even more than the day."⁴⁵ Neglecting study at night might cause, figuratively, the "house to be eventually devoured by fire."⁴⁶ Indeed, self deprivation almost to the point of asceticism is deemed a prerequisite to the intensive study of the Torah. Only those are worthy of preserving the holy precepts "who work hard and suppress the needs of their bodies always, not allowing sleep to their eyes nor slumber to their⁴⁷ eyelids."⁴⁸

The Code also seeks to stimulate effort by warning of unhappy consequences of slackness and neglect:

> Whoever is able to occupy himself with the Torah and does not, and whoever reads or studies and [then] turns to this wordly foolishness and puts away his study and neglects it is like [those] who have "despised the words of the Lord."⁴⁹

While the Code attaches high value to the study of the Torah, it also recognizes the importance of religious observances and charitable deeds in the service of God.⁵⁰ Effort in these areas is stimulated by precept, example, and promise of reward. It is a duty to be early at the synagogue "so that one may be counted among the first ten."⁵¹

A person should feel such urge to be at the synagogue that he should actually quicken his pace; this is permissible even on the Sabbath when fast and strenuous walking is generally forbidden.⁵² Similarly, one should hasten to perform any charitable deed.⁵³

The noble actions of sages are set up as examples to be followed by all. It was customary for one of the greatest of sages to leave money clandestinely on the doorsteps of the poor, for "thus it is worth doing."⁵⁴ Love and veneration of the Torah are inculcated by the example of the sages in kissing the phylacteries before and after their use in prayers.⁵⁵ And it is told of King David that he never slept beyond "sixty inhalations and exhalations . . . during the day,"⁵⁶ as an example of devotion to work and study.

Inculcating habits of prayer is deemed of utmost importance, and its practice is encouraged by the statement that one who prays: "shall be rewarded as if he had read the Torah."⁵⁷ Thus, through prayer, even the illiterate may acquire merit on a par with the learned. But the reward of prayer in the morning is greater if begun with the sunrise than if started later in the day.⁵⁸

Learning by Doing—Directed Activity

Horne states that interest and effort can be secured by combining both into action, that " . . .the child must do religious things, whether at first he understands their full import or not . . . better his doing one religious deed than learning many religious truths."⁵⁹

The Code is aware of this principle of religious education. Children are taught to utter "the complete blessing"[60] as part of their study, although the prayer, per se, was said in vain because a direct need was absent. To add dignity and verisimilitude to the practice, the listeners were urged to answer "amen."[61]

The learning by doing frequently involved participation[62] in family and communal activities. Minors who are not obliged to learn certain prayers or religious practices until they reach the age of thirteen, are permitted and even urged to practice these in the acquisition of a good religious education even before they understand their full significance properly. Thus, the father is urged to buy phylacteries for his son while the latter is still a minor, and to train him in their use.[63] The minor should also be induced to use the lulav,[64] and practice lighting the Chanukah candles.[65] This dictum is carried to the point where an adult is permitted to have a minor say grace in his place.[66]

Learning by Doing—Self-Activity

According to Klapper, "...whatever appears to us as useful and necessary in society calls forth an expression of our self-activity and prompts to action, for interest is an active attitude toward experience."[67] Closely related to the principle of learning by doing under guidance, is the principle of self-activity. By precept and example, as well as by attaching high social value to religious observances, the Code encourages self-activity in both children and adults.

> Minors [should] say grace after meals by themselves [if they are in a company of three].[68]
>
> And where it is customary for minors to say the evening prayers before the Ark at the conclusion of the Sabbath, that practice should be defended.[69]
>
> The RaSH,[70] personally, was accustomed to participate and to stimulate others in preparing the matzah [i.e., specially supervised and prepared unleavened bread]; each one himself should attend to this mitzvah.[71]
>
> Regardless of the number of servants one may have, he should arise early on Friday and do something to prepare for the Sabbath. Rabbi Ḥisda used to cut the vegetables into very fine pieces, and Rabbah and Rabbi Yosef used to cut wood, . . . Rabbi Zeira used to kindle the fire . . . and from them everyone should learn. . . .[72]

Self-activity in religious matters—and we must keep in mind that the orientation of the Code is religious—is expected to be carried out carefully and in a reverent spirit. In composing one's own prayer, one must be careful, alert, and of sound judgment; else we prefer "that he concentrate on the three [already established] daily prayers."[73]

Individual Differences

According to Curoe, "Individual differences will necessitate adjustment in method and rate of progress."[74] And he goes on to state: "Flexibility is that kind of elasticity which makes it possible for each child to proceed through the experiences of the curriculum at a tempo commensurate with his ability."[75] The Code deals only incidentally with the problem of individual differences in the ability to learn, and takes into consideration both special aptitude and the problem of the learner.

In the Code, opportunity for advanced education is to be provided for a boy who gives evidence of special aptitude, even if giving him the opportunity means depriving his father of formal instruction. Thus we read:

> He needed to learn and his son needed to learn, but he cannot afford to provide education for both. If both are equally intelligent, he has preferences over his son. If his son proves more discerning and intelligent he has preference over his father.[76]

The problem of the slow student is also referred to. He is to be given at least the opportunity to learn what he can on the elementary level. Even if the child does not have the aptitude for learning to read, he is not to be removed from the school, but is to "sit with the others; perhaps he will learn."[77] Beyond more exposure to instruction, the Code advocates honest self-evaluation on the part of the student, and patience and diligence on the part of both student and teacher. The student need not be ashamed of the fact that his classmates learn more quickly, for such attitude will prevent him from learning anything[78] in the Beth Hamidrash.[79]

> [It is] not a shamefaced person [who] is apt to learn, nor [is it] an impatient person [who is] fitted to teach.[80]

A teacher shall not become angry with students when they fail to understand the subject matter; he shall repeat the explanation until it is grasped by them. Nor shall the student fail to admit his lack of understanding but should demand repeatedly further instruction.[81]

The Code, therefore, does not expect all students to learn at the same rate; nor does it accept as adequate mere learning by rote; the crucial importance of understanding in the learning process is stressed, and tempo is to be adjusted to achieve understanding.

Memory

The Code advocated the method of repetition[82] as a means of acquiring knowledge. This method is also recommended for memorizing material after its meaning has been grasped.

> Even though one hears the entire weekly portion of the Torah every Sabbath in public one is dutybound to read for himself thrice each week the portion for that week.[83]
>
> Each one is dutybound to study continuously until the day of one's death,[84] because by failing to do so, he may forget the contents of the Torah.[85]

A physical reminder is deemed useful for stimulating the memory. For example, even in the Diaspora, when baking a challah,[86] one is to set aside a piece of the dough from which the challah is made so that "the laws concerning challah should not be forgotten by the people of Israel."[87]

The principle of any mnemonic system is to create some kind of association, usually accidental, with the idea to be remembered.[88] The Code provides a mnemonic system wherever possible. In the case of *terefa*, i.e., forbidden meat, the Code lists three words, the initials of which are to remind one of the eight reasons why meat may be forbidden. These are: D'n, Ḥn'k, and nph'sh, and they mean "judge," "choked," and "soul" (life) respectively, which in turn are the initials for the following words:

Derussah	דרוסה	—animal clawed by another animal
Nekuvah	נקובה	—punctured
Ḥasurah	חסורה	—missing parts of limbs or body
Netulah	נטולה	—an animal with destroyed or missing organ in body[89]
Keruah	קרועה	—torn
Nefulah	נפולה	—prematurely born
P[h]sukah	פסוקה	—interrupted slaughtering
Shevurah	שבורה	—broken bone[90]

Inculcation of Right Conduct

Klapper further states: "We must develop in the child habits of right conduct and inculcate proper attitudes. These accumulated tendencies form a powerful stock of inhibitions so that when a wrong act is willed the whole nervous system rises in revolt."[91]

The Code tries to inculcate attitudes which are primarily religious and ethical. One is abjured to have an attitude of willingness, even eagerness, in the service of God:

> Let him strengthen himself like a lion to rise in the morning to the service of his Creator so that he may be the awakener of the dawn.[92]

One is taught the duty of fulfilling one's commitments, even commitments to oneself. Thus, if a resolution has been made to study daily a certain number of pages of the Torah and the assignment was not completed during the day, there is an obligation to complete the task immediately at night.[93]

There must be an attitude of reverence in all religious observances. In praying, a person must concentrate on the meaning of the words he utters. He must say the words attentively as if he were addressing royalty; indeed, in prayer we are addressing the King of Kings who is aware of one's innermost thoughts.[94] Very pious men are accustomed to seclude themselves and to concentrate on their prayers until they reach the stage of 'all-soulness' beyond rationality. . . . And one should think of things that humble the heart."[95]

An attitude of special reverence is expected in using the name of God and in performing ritualistic acts. If, during the process of writing the scroll of the Torah, he is about to inscribe the ineffable Name, he shall not interrupt his work even to reply to a question[96] of the King of Israel.

Reverence for the Torah is almost personified. If while walking one sees someone carrying a Torah, he is to stop until the Torah reaches its destination or is carried out of sight.[97]

One method of inculcating habits of reverent religious observance is through dignified behavior—repeated ritualistic acts.[98] It is customary "to put on becoming garments for the synagogue."[99] On the eve of the Sabbath, one is to use a soft voice in ordering someone in the family to light candles.[100] And one is to tidy up the house before the Sabbath arrives so as to find his home "in order and neatness when returning from the synagogue."[101]

The Code enjoins an attitude of joy and generosity, especially during the holidays; gift-giving is suggested as a means of achieving this attitude. The children are to be treated to roasted grain and nuts, and "for the wife one is to buy dresses and jewelry according to his ability."[102]

Other attitudes to be developed, more secular in their implications, are, fairness and good will, justice, generosity—especially in giving charity—and self-reliance.[103]

One may distribute gifts to members of the family on the Sabbath by drawing lots. However, it is incumbent on him that the value of the gifts be equal, so that they will be accepted with good grace; the objective shall be to obviate feelings of jealousy among the recipients. Even on weekdays it is forbidden to draw lots in the distribution of gifts of unequal value. Such a lottery device is similar to gambling and dice.

The attitude toward charity is reflected in the following passage: "Never is a man the poorer for giving charity, nor does any evil occur to him through it. . . .[104] But a person should prefer deprivation of customary Sabbath foods to dependence on charity. And performing repulsive work is better than dependence.[105]

Social Development

In addition to developing the physical and mental capacities of the individual, education is also concerned with his development of proper social attitudes towards groups, first the family and then the community at large.[106] He is to be taught the need for integrating himself with the community by serving as a leader, if capable, and the need for participating in the activities of the synagogue and of charitable groups. Other desirable social amenities are encouraged, for instance, the visiting of the sick,[107] and the accompanying of the dead to the cemetery.[108] Moroever, compulsory means are to be used, if necessary, to safeguard the proper attitudes towards the educational ideals of the community.

The father is obliged to hire a tutor for his son. And if he does not hire a tutor, even though he has the means, the court has the right to attach his goods in order to defray the cost of education.[109] Knowledge of his people's history and traditions[110] is desirable to foster and inspire emulation and a spirit of sacrifice for the group.

Respect for Parents

One of the first principles of Jewish social education is respect for one's parents. It is based on the Fifth Commandment—"Honor thy father and thy mother."[111] And it extends through the entire social organization of Jewish communities.

Reverence for parents is adjured.[112] Many examples of such adjuration may be cited: One should not use his father's proper name in speaking about him but should use the phrase, "my father, sir";[113] one should not occupy the place his father uses, at home or in the synagogue; nor should one contradict one's father's opinion even by saying, "I think I am right, father."[114]

It is not enough that one feed, dress, and serve his father; the attitude must be one of love and friendliness. Otherwise the son's actions merit punishment.[115] Even if the parents should apply physical punishment, the child is not permitted to show them irreverence. Even if the son were to preside over a public meeting dressed in most costly garments, and his parents tore his garments and spat in his face, he must submit quietly without rejoinder.[116]

Harsh indeed is the punishment for insulting one's parents. The court is to punish severely anyone who degrades his parents by word or gesture; such transgressors are cursed by God.[117]

But even reverence and obedience for one's father must give way to obedience to the Torah. A child must not transgress commandments of the Law even at the behest of his parents.[118] And it is recognized that such high ideals of respect and reverence for parents may make life difficult for children. Therefore parents are forbidden to impose unreasonable obligations on their children, and are enjoined not to be unduly sensitive where their honor is involved.[119]

As previously mentioned, honoring one's parents has further implications. One is to honor one's step-parents,[120] one's father-in-law,[121] and one's elder brothers.[122]

Respect for Teachers and Elders

Respect for and obedience to one's teacher ranks at least on a par with respect for and obedience to one's parents. It is a person's duty, child or adult, to honor and revere a teacher;[123] one is to show extreme courtesy in his greeting by saying: "Peace be upon you, my teacher."[124] One is not to sit down in the presence of the teacher unless told to do so.[125] And to oppose one's teacher is equivalent to opposing the Divine Presence.[126] Respect is to be shown to all elderly people, particularly the learned man and sages, even if they are younger and not one's teacher. Such respect is to be shown by arising in their presence.[127]

Training for Leadership

Lay Leadership

From the various regulations in the Shulchan Aruch it is evident that criteria for lay leadership exist, although no explicit principles relating to preparation for lay leadership are to be found. Such criteria are, in the main, personal traits such as piety, honesty, reliability, and general ability, to be supplemented, if possible, by sufficient learning in the Torah.[128] Since the principles underlying Jewish education, explicit and implicit in the Shulchan Aruch, aim at developing the qualities mentioned, we may state that the same principles function also in developing lay leadership. In a certain sense this attitude is comparable to that implied in certain ideals of general education, namely, the development of basic qualities of character, the development of a sense of duty to society,[129] and the awakening of stimuli to learning. The program is thus a prerequisite for all youth—a truly democratic ideal. Moses expressed this spirit when he said, "... Would God that all the Lord's people were prophets...."[130] Those most capable and devoted to public service would naturally gravitate toward religious and lay leadership, because serving the public is deemed extremely meritorious: for "Whoever serves the needs of the public is as if he busied himself with [the study of] the Torah."[131]

It will be sufficient, we believe, to cite here a few instances that indicate some of the additional qualities required of leaders. Of these, a deep sense of responsibility for one's utterances is of paramount importance. The Code exhorts: "Let it not become a custom with you to make vows...."[132] Again, the community is itself enjoined to be watchful in appointing only such to public service as will be concerned with the public welfare.[133]

Leadership involves the quality of tact and consideration even for the lowliest members of the group. Thus, collectors of charity are asked to be discreet in the collection and the distribution of donations.[134]

Leaders are told that they must have a sense of humility.

> It is not befitting a leader to burden the people by purposefully passing through their midst so that they stand up before him in respect, but he should seek a way so that not many would have to stand up. And if he can find a way of bypassing them, it is to his credit.[135]

Moses was praised for being the most meek of men on earth.[136] Arrogant judges were warned they would not be deprived of having a learned son.[137] Honesty and piety are stressed in the selection of supervisors.[138]

The implication of qualities desired in leaders may be deduced also from the qualities requisite in laymen who serve as members of a court. These qualities are: "wisdom, humility, fear, hatred for money, love for truth, being loved by the people, and possessing a good reputation."[139]

Responsibility to the Community

In joining a new community, the newcomer is expected to conform to local customs even if they differ from those of his former community.[140] In all matters the member is duty-bound to abide by the decisions of the majority of the town's people.[141]

Refraining from participation in public life is deemed a grievous fault.[142] The individual is encouraged to express his opinion in problems concerning the group. In the congregation, the individual has the right to voice objection and say, "I do not want this man to be the cantor."[143]

One of the sacred obligations of the individual is to share in the responsibility for the education of the poor which is to begin with early childhood. One is "obliged to participate in the charity chest"[144] even if he has lived but thirty days in the community. Although the requirement for compulsory formal education for boys does not extend beyond the elementary level, the community is exhorted to provide for the advanced schooling of the poor children who show capabilities for further study.[145]

The community is also duty-bound to appoint charity collectors, "men of renown and honesty,"[146] and one is not to contribute to the communal charity chest unless he knows that the man in charge is honest and capable of performing his duties.[147] Before prayer one should contribute to charity, even it be the smallest coin.[148] The recipient of charity is encouraged to give "from what others give him."[149] If one gives less than he can afford, the court may compel him to give the amount assessed by the civic authority, even to the extent of seizing the required donation.[150] Rich and poor are urged to give charity, for it is written, ". . . thou shalt not harden thine heart, nor shut thine hand. . . ."[151]

Respect for Historical Events

The principle of respect for Jewish historical events as a means of intensifying the religious sentiment is an important phase of the development of the individual. Commemoration of historical events are entwined with their observance as Holy Days, and they have strong religious significance.[152] One is not only to observe these events in celebration at home, but in the communal ceremonies and prayers in the synagogue. Such observances are compulsory, both at home and in the synagogue. Several instances may serve to illustrate this point.

The story of the Exodus is celebrated in the Holy Days of Passover for a period of eight days. Special communal prayers are held in the synagogue. At home, the event is celebrated by the performance of the Seder[153] and the use of special foods, drinks, and ceremonial rituals. The story of the Exodus is to precede and follow the meal at the Seder; one must narrate the stories until overcome by sleep.[154]

During the night and day of the ninth of Ab,[155] the congregation " . . . sits on the floor around one lighted candle . . . to read the Book of Lamentations."[156]

The Maccabean victory is celebrated during the Feast of Lights, and one is urged to light the candles facing public places;[157] indeed, "One should be very careful to light the candles of Chanukah."[158]

On Purim, "even the study of the Torah is set aside"[159] to hear the reading of the Book of Esther, in commemoration of the victory over Haman. Thus past events and their religious connotations are united as a chain to tie the individual to his group.

Maintaining the Religious Spirit

The Torah is considered the very foundation on which the superstructure of the Jewish life rests. The Torah contains in itself all knowledge basic to the good life, individually and collectively.

Knowledge of the Torah and obedience to its precepts as expounded in the commentaries are vital for the very existence of the Jewish community and the integration of the individual with it. "All the Jews are united in fellowship." All are bound together into a spiritual social group by sharing in religious observances and by following common ethical precepts. No one is permitted to have an attitude of disinterest towards another's welfare; penance is demanded of one who fails to ask his friend how he fares or who vows not to lend him his utensils.[160] Lack of participation in community activities can result in stigmatization and excommunication.[161]

An important principle of education, therefore, is the inculcation of the attitude of devotion towards the Torah and the glorious rewards of mastering its contents. Knowlege of the Torah is essential for developing lifelong habits of religious behavior.[162] All doubts as to correct conduct are resolved by reference to some phrase in the Torah. Eternal life is gained through religious performances which presuppose knowledge of the Torah.[163]

Study of the Torah is therefore imposed on all, rich and poor.

> Whosoever neglects the Torah out of riches is bound to neglect it out of poverty; and whosoever maintains the Torah in poverty is bound to maintain it also in riches.[164]

While the Torah is still a source of moral education, teachers are enjoined not to teach the Torah to spiritually unworthy students until they have been guided to the proper moral path.[165] Indeed, the community is enjoined not to accept the services of a rabbi or scholar who lacks piety and devotion to the laws of the Torah.[166]

The ideal in Jewish religious education to serve God and to study the Law is embodied in the following commandments:

> [The teacher] should sit and teach the entire day and a little during the night in order to train them [the children] to study day and night.[167]
>
> It is incumbent upon each Jewish man to study the Torah be he poor or rich, healthy or sick, young or old. Even the beggar who knocks on the door, even a married man must set aside special times day and night for the study of the Torah, as it is written that 'thou shalt meditate therein day and night.'[168]

Reverence for the Torah is another principle underlying the preservation of the religious spirit. The Torah is personified and given supreme homage. One is to stand up in the presence of the scroll when it is taken out of the ark. Holy Scriptures should be saved from fire even on the Sabbath, regardless of the languages in which they are written;[169] and one who sees them consumed by fire should rend his garments in mourning.[170] Fragments of Scripture should be buried and not be cast away as trash.[171] Cohabitation is forbidden in a house where there are Holy Scriptures, unless "separated by a wall."[172] Reverence for the Law is transmitted to the teacher of the Torah. "...let the... reverence for thy master [be] like the fear of heaven."[173]

Reverence is attached to ritual performances to emphasize the religious spirit. For example, to assure wine for the Seder ritual, the poorest are enjoined to sell their garments, borrow, or hire out in service, if necessary.[174]

Social Adjustment between Jews and Non-Jews

Jewish attitudes towards non-Jews, as toward their own brethren, has its roots in principles and laws found in or deduced from the Torah.[175] The Code provides that the relations between Jews and non-Jews are to be guided by customs and traditions of both groups. However, in cases where Biblical principles are in opposition to accepted usage, the former takes precedence. Thus a Jew is permitted to lend his utensils to a non-Jew even though they are to be used on the Sabbath, although he may not lend a draft animal because his animal must rest on the Sabbath.

According to the Biblical precept, "We are not commanded to keep utensils at rest on the Sabbath."[176] The Code says Jews are forbidden to have their phylacteries written by a non-Jew, or even by a Jewish woman or minor, for the Torah has commanded "and ye [the adult male] shall . . . write them."[177]

In general, business dealings among fellow-Jews and non-Jews are to be conducted on the same ethical basis. A Jew, in dealings with his fellow man, should refrain from practices which lead to litigations; he should "avoid enmity, robbery, and false oaths."[178] One is strongly warned against committing any kind of fraud or deception:

> Just as there exists deception in transactions, so it exists in words, and deception in words is even harsher than in money, for in the former case it is not given to accounting . . . and whoever cries [to God] for being deceived by words is immediately answered.[179]

Similarly, in their business dealings the people are warned not to cheat on weight and measures on penalty of being fined "in any way the court sees fit."[180] Indeed, this measure refers to cheating "a Jew or even a non-Jew."[181]

Only where religious precepts are involved does the Code authorize any different mode of conduct. A Jew may permit a non-Jew to carry his money for him on the Sabbath; his own animal, however, may not do so but must rest on the Sabbath.[182] Such distinctions do not in any sense indicate a lack of consideration for non-Jews. In fact, Jews are required to honor and lend a "supporting hand" to a non-Jew.[183] Thus, Jews are required to "declare a fast if an epidemic rages among non-Jews."[184]

Respect for non-Jewish dignitaries is encouraged; the Jew is required to pronounce a blessing upon seeing a learned non-Jew[185] or a non-Jewish King.[186]

Stealing from a Jew or a non-Jew is equally forbidden.[187] Wherever religious precepts permit, a non-Jew is considered an equal. Thus, a non-Jewish servant in a Jewish home is permitted to cook meat, if the servant knows the ritual required in preparing the meat for cooking.[188]

Partnership with non-Jews is encouraged whenever such partnership helps fulfill Biblical commandments. Thus, to avoid the difficulties involved in looking after the firstling of an ox, of a sheep, or a goat, such partnership is encouraged.[189]

Jewish Attitude Towards Government

Basically, the same principles that guide Jewish conduct toward non-Jewish neighbors also guide Jews in fulfilling their obligation toward government, namely cooperation, responsibility, and loyalty. All laws of the Civil Government "are binding."[190] However, if principles of religion are involved, then "the [official's] order should be weighed against our religion."[191] Thus, if a Jew were excommunicated and the [non-Jewish] official decreed punishment upon those adhering to the order of excommunication, it would depend on the cause leading to the excommunication as to whether or not the pious Jew is to abide by the religious edict.

During Caro's time, when Jews had their own courts, Jews were exhorted to use them for purposes of bringing lawsuits.[192] Lawsuits between Jews and non-Jews were referred to non-Jewish courts only if the non-Jew was opposed to the rulings of a Jewish court.[193]

Attitude Towards Secular Studies

The principle of maintaining the religious spirit is foremost in determining the Jewish attitude towards secular education. Thus, on the Sabbath and on holidays, only the Torah may be studied.[194] Some liberal rabbis have permitted use of the astrolabe and the reading of books of medicine and science.[195] But secular literature, regardless of the language in which it is written, is forbidden at all times if the contents are deemed harmful to the development of moral attitudes.[196] Hebrew education strongly stresses moral values and aims "to bring man into conscious relationship with God."[197] Thus, the reading of any literature that tends to evoke lust, immoral action, or an attitude of cynicism is forbidden since this is tantamount to sitting "in the seat of scoffers."[198]

In general, we may say that secular education is encouraged when the principles taught tend to strengthen Biblical teachings. Secular literature may touch on any scientific or ethical material consistent with Biblical teachings. But where secular content is in disagreement with Biblical doctrine, measures should be taken to avoid such literature.

Educational Practices in the Shulchan Aruch

Having discussed the educational principles expounded in the Shulchan Aruch, we now proceed to a discussion of the educational practices.

Early Childhood Education

At what age should one beging to teach his son? As soon as the child starts to talk,[199] the father should begin to teach him the declaration: "Moses gave us the Torah. . . ."[200] etc., and the first sentence of the Sh'ma.[201] Thereafter he should teach him, little by little,[202] until he is about six or even seven years old, at which age he is to bring him to a teacher to begin his formal studies.

We note that the age for beginning education depends upon the child's ability to talk and, presumably, to learn. Before the child enters the school he is to be exposed to the religious influences and practices of the family. The father is responsible for this phase of his child's training. He is also to teach the youngster the rudiments of Hebrew reading.

The Basic Curriculum

In the previous paragraphs we noted that stress was laid upon teaching the Bible to the child; the Bible was basic at every state of education. The parent was obligated to pay for this instruction, if necessary. The Shulchan Aruch states: "If it was the custom of the town for a teacher to take a fee, then he must pay for his [son's] instruction until the boy reads the entire Torah."[203] If the father is able to pay, he must have his son taught Mishnah, Talmud, the Hallachah or legal decisions, and the non-legal elements of Rabbinic literature.[204]

The foregoing ruling again reveals that the only subject of concern to the community in the education of their children was the teaching of the Torah.

Home

> Children should be admitted to formal schooling only when they are fully five years old. However, if the child is in delicate health, he is not to begin his schooling before he is fully six years.[205]

It is clear that the home took the place of the present-day nursery kindergarten until the child was five, or at the most, if the child was in delicate health, six. The father was expected to prepare the child for school, and it was his responsibility to do so thoroughly and to the best of his ability. Rabbi Moses Isserles advises that the child should be familiarized with the Hebrew alphabet before he reaches his third year.[206]

Intensity of Learning

The teacher is to teach his pupils the whole day and a little into the night in order to train them to study by day and night.[207] It should be pointed out that this passage refers to the teaching of the Torah. The practice of studying by day and night is still pursued to some extent among the very pious.

Children should not be dismissed from their studies earlier than the scheduled hour except for the eve of the Sabbath or the eve of festivals and holy days.[208] This regulation serves to emphasize the value attached to Jewish education in the Shulchan Aruch, especially the study of the Torah. Earnestness of purpose and intensity in the quality of study applied to teacher and pupil alike.

Classroom Discipline

Discipline, usually a problem with minors, is discussed very briefly: "The teacher must not strike his pupil vengefully or harshly, nor is he to beat him with whips or a stick. He may use only a small strap."[209] Today corporal punishment is prohibited in many school systems. Where it is permitted, it is also regulated along principles similar to those in the Code.

The Slow Learner

The problem of the backward pupil is not unusual. Although the Code is not explicit in making a distinction between what we today know as a mentally defective child from what may be considered a slow learner, the Shulchan Aruch offers the following treatment:

> Even a child that does not know how to read is not to be dismissed from the classroom. He is to be permitted to sit with the other students in the hope that he may eventually understand.[210]

The Learning Process

The Code was also concerned with the students' learning process. The student is advised to be frank in admitting that he fails to understand a given passage and to ask questions, even if the teacher becomes angry. We read:

> And the student should not say "I understand" when in reality he did not understand. And he should ask again and again. Should the teacher become angry, let the student say, "Master, it is the Torah that I am studying, and I must learn it even though I am slow to grasp."[211]

The Code takes cognizance of the imporance of concentration in learning. The student is advised to avoid any practice that might interfere with his concentrating on his studies. The Code urges extreme effort in order to achieve optimum results. The Code maintains that

> Knowledge of the Torah will not take root in one who is lax in his studies nor in those who study while they take their pleasures or while eating or drinking, but only with him who is ready to give his life for the sake of the Torah, who constantly mortifies his body and abstains from sleep to devote himself to the study of the Torah.[212]

The Code further advises the learner to read aloud when studying, so as to stimulate his power of retention. The student is also advised that silent reading results in forgetting quickly. The Code states:

One who makes use of his voice when studying will retain what he learns, while the one that reads silently will forget quickly.[213]

The Code stresses the importance of the student's character and attitude as prerequisites for the study of the Torah, to prevent possible abuse of knowledge. This is understandable in light of the fact that the layman usually looked to the rabbi for advice, and the rabbi's abuse of his position could have serious consequences. The Code therefore warned:

> The Torah is not to be taught to a student whose behavior is improper.[214] Such a person is to be corrected and guided to righteousness. Only after he is examined and found worthy is he to be admitted to the school and taught there.[215]

The Teacher

According to the Code, the qualifications for a good teacher are of prime importance. The basic motivation for becoming a teacher should be the precept: "And thou shalt teach them diligently unto thy children."[216] The Shulchan Aruch states:

> Let one not say: "Just as I had to pay for [my] instruction, so will I teach for pay" but he should teach others without thought of pay.[217]

The elementary school teacher's marital status is the concern of the community, and regarding this the Shulchan Aruch provides that:

> One who is unmarried may not be a teacher of young children since it is customary for the mothers to bring their children to school. However, it is not necessary that his wife stay with him at school. She may remain at home while the teacher teaches in the customary place.[218]

Apparently, this ruling applies only to teachers of the very young, and the reason for it is obvious.

A parallel ruling forbids the teaching of the young by women. "A woman should not be a teacher of young children since it is customary for the fathers to bring their children to school."[219] This ruling is of interest for it implies that there were women interested in teaching.

Regarding standards and competition in the teaching profession, the Code says:

> A man from among the neighbors bordering on a common courtyard, who wishes to become an elementary school teacher, may not be

> prevented by his neighbor from doing so. Similarly, if another elementary school teacher comes to open a school near the first one, either to attract other pupils or even to attract the pupils of the first teacher, he may not be prevented from doing so. For it is said, "The Lord delights in seeing the Torah gloriously increased for the sake of His righteousness."[220]
>
> Where there is a teacher for the young children and another appears who is superior, the first is to be removed and the second appointed in his place.[221]

The Shulchan Aruch expresses a preference in methodology and approach:

> If there are two teachers, one who emphasizes [at length] but does not teach the pupils to understand the subject matter read, while the other one emphasizes accuracy and comprehension, but does not cover much ground, preference is given to the one who emphasizes accuracy in comprehension.[222]

This passage implies that the educational method was the concern of the community. This is made even clearer when we consider that one of the major goals in learning was the correct interpretation of the Bible.

The teacher's character and influence upon his pupils was a matter of concern to the community. Youngsters do imitate their elders, and certainly imitate their teacher with whom they spend a large portion of their time. The Code expresses this concern about the moral character of the teacher in the following words:

> A teacher who does not walk in the right path, even though he is very learned and the people need him, should not be emulated until he mends his ways.[223]

Regarding the responsibility of the teacher, the Code says:

> A teacher of the young who leaves his pupils [alone] and goes out of the room, does some other work with them, or is lax in teaching, is considered as one whom Jeremiah condemns: "Cursed be he who does the work of the Lord deceitfully." (*Jeremiah* XLVIII, 10]. Therefore, one should not appoint a teacher who is not God-fearing as well as punctilious.[224]

We note from the foregoing passage that the teacher's qualifications depend, in large measure, upon his attitude towards religion. Of no less importance is the manner in which he carries out his responsibility toward the pupils.

The Code views the contractual relationship specifically in the case of teaching as in any other work. The teacher's pay was protected or forfeited like that of any other worker's. The Shulchan Aruch provides that when one hires a teacher for his son and the son falls sick, the employer is liable for the tuition fee if the illness is not chronic. If it is chronic, and the teacher being in the same town is aware of the circumstances, the loss is the teacher's. If it is a chronic ailment of which the teacher is not aware, not having resided in the same town, the loss is to be the parents'.[225]

The Shulchan Aruch also states that a teacher should not hire out his services into a household where another tutor is already employed.[226]

We are also informed that if the wife hired a teacher for her son and the husband knew of it and did not object, the assumption is that he gave his consent to her act. However, if he protested promptly, then her act is null and void.[227] This, again, protects the teacher's position.

Adult Education

It has been a practice in Jewish religious life for the adult to continue his study of the Torah according to a definite plan. This is expressed in the Shulchan Aruch by the following ruling which reads in part:

> One is obliged to divide his studies into three parts . . . for example, if he is an artisan who devoted three hours to his work and nine hours for the study of the Torah, three of these are to be given over to the study of the Written Law, three to the Oral Law, and three hours to analysis of his studies.[228]

The Education of Women

The man, who is considered capable of learning and to be able to penetrate into the deeper aspects of the Torah, is expected to study it. A woman, however, is not required to study Torah. If she does so, she earns merit, but not as much as a man. And even if she acquires such merit, our sages have commanded that a man should not teach his daughter Torah, since most women are not considered able to grasp the intricacies of the Law, and she may apply her learning in a superficial manner. That is why the sages have said, "He who teaches his daughter Torah, it is as if he had taught her folly."[229] However, this refers only to the Oral Law, which encompasses the rabbinic works. The Written Law, on the other hand, is not to be taught *ab initio*—but if he did teach it to her, he has not committed a wrong.

From the foregoing we note that the Code advocates only the more practical aspects of education for women, such as would fit them to meet their obligations as wives, mothers, and members of the community.

CHAPTER III

ANALYSIS OF THE BASIC EDUCATIONAL PRINCIPLES AND PRACTICES IN THE SHULCHAN ARUCH IN RELATION TO MODERN EDUCATION

We have thus far discussed a number of educational principles and practices found in the Shulchan Aruch.[1] We shall now attempt to analyze them in terms of modern education.

Physical Development

Concerning physical development, we observed that the Code considers any phase of physical development as secondary to spiritual development. In modern educational institutions, physical education occupies a prominent place in the curriculum.[2] It is an end in itself. General education, emphasizing the needs of the present, gives much greater priority to physical development of the child than the Shulchan Aruch with its emphasis on religion.

Rest, Health and Hygiene, Food, and Recreation[3]

Certain aspects of physical care, however, are regarded as of primary importance in the Code. We noted, for instance, that "anyone who neglects his own illness is comparable to a murderer."[4] Similarly, we observed that the Code stresses the value of bodily cleanliness and the importance of inculcating hygienic habits in people. Thus we note that "the offering of drink to another from a cup from which one has drunk previously is to be avoided."[5] In the Code, as in secular education, good food habits are encouraged. The Code urges one to eat moderately and to develop proper habits of elimination.[6] One is required in the Code to wash before meals and on other occasions, as a means of preventing infection and contamination. This, of course, is in line with modern hygiene concepts.[7]

The Code also indicates that in order to develop properly the student's character, and to direct his religious training, it is necessary to arouse interest in his own ethical improvement. He must learn to keep the commandments by actually practicing them on his own level. This should develop right attitudes and correct patterns of behavior by emulating the conduct of sages, teachers, and parents. The purpose of study should not be merely to acquire knowlege for its own sake, but should lead to the acquisition of proper attitudes and habits of conduct.[8] In modern education character training is considered to be an aim of prime importance.[9] Thus, both the Code and contemporary education can be seen to have a common pragmatic aim—learning to live the good life.

Arousing Interest and Stimulating Effort

In the Code the learner is motivated by being reminded constantly of the values in learning and following the precepts of theTorah.[10] The reward for learning and the punishment for not doing so are stressed. Study is also intended to bring about intelligent religious practice and observance.

In modern education, motivation plays an important role. The student is encouraged to greater effort by recognition of the values of his studies as the latter relate to his growth both as an individual and as a member of the community.[11] Reward rather than punishment is to be stressed.[12]

We have noted that the Code stresses learning by doing, or learning through activity. Thus, minors are encouraged to participate in synagogue prayers and services, not formally, but under the supervision of their elders. The Code states that children should participate in the observance of ritual such as the lighting of candles on Chanukah, the Feast of Lights, and during the celebration of other festivals and holy days.[13]

In modern education, too, we note that study is to be related to activity or a project, to be carried on under supervision. Darcy expresses this idea well in his statement that "under normal conditions, learning is a product and reward of occupation with subject matter."[14] Anderson points out that supervised activities should aim to develop within the student a responsibility toward community needs and prepare him for leadership.[15]

Learning by Doing—Self-Activity

The Code advocates a degree of self-activity when it urges the individual to imitate the practices of eminent rabbis and sages who would themselves carry out chores in preparation for the Sabbath and the various festivals.[16] In modern education, too, it is urged that learning should include various experiences such as publishing a school paper, visiting places of cultural interest, and other activities.[17] There is thus another instance of identity in viewpoint between the Code and present-day education.

Individual Differences

The Code recognizes the evidence of individual differences.[18] The approach of the Code differs, however, from that of modern education. The Code, for instance, advocates that the slow learner should sit in with the others, "perhaps he will learn."[19] In modern education, however, individual differences are taken into consideration in the process of learning, and students are grouped according to their needs. In the words of Schorling, "If the pupil is to find real zest in the task, the hill to be ascended must be as steep and as long as he can climb under his own power."[20]

Memory

Repetition and association as a means of developing memory are stressed in the Code,[21] which, accordingly, suggests several mnemonic patterns as previously noted. Horne urges that modern education make greater use of both memorization and association.[22] Schorling suggests that repetition and drill be used and that the subject studied be made interesting to the student.[23] It would seem that the Shulchan Aruch again is in line with the views expressed by outstanding American educational authorities.

Inculcation of Right Conduct

The Code, as would be expected, regards character training as a permanent goal of religious education. It urges the inculcation of right conduct and proper attitudes.[24] John Dewey feels that "unless the learning which accrues in the regular course of study affects character, it is futile to conceive the moral end as the unifying and culminating end of education."[25] Brubacher remarks that education is a process in which good habits are achieved.[26]

Social Development
Respect for Parents, Teachers, and Elders

The Code proposes the inculcation of proper social attitudes by training a child to obey his parents and to respect and honor his teachers and elders.[27] In modern education, it is urged that the child develop characteristics of obedience and respect. Symonds[28] points out that parents can teach their children obedience by being firm, consistent, requiring order and routine, and by imposing fair demands on the child. Havighurst[29] points out that by participating in social institutions, the child develops loyalty.

Training for Leadership

In the Code[30] preparation for leadership is incidental to the development of character attributes. Leadership must demonstrate good habits, and such personal traits as piety, honesty, reliability, and general ability. In fact, these are the justifications for determining whether one should or should not be entrusted with a responsible position.[31] In modern education the development of personal qualities such as intellectual integrity, honesty, and sincerity are of basic importance in leadership training.[32] Activities designed to produce within the student a sense of responsibility and leadership are urged.[33]

Responsibility to the Community

The Code underscores the responsibility of the individual to the community by urging him to abide by the decisions of the majority, to voice an opinion in matters concerning the group, and to participate in communal expenses even when he himself is a recipient of charity.[34] In modern education an important goal is to imbue the student with a sense of responsibility toward the community. Butler feels strongly on this point when he says: "How can a truly religious life or any other life which is worthy . . . shrink from entering into social responsibility?"[35]

Respect for Historical Events

The Code requires the celebration of historical events as a means of intensifying religious sentiment, and enhancing the appreciation of historical events[36] associated with the various festivals. In modern secular education, it is urged that the students participate in social and cultural life and be aware of the history of their city, state, and nation, which may tend to improve citizenship.[37]

Social Adjustment Between Jews and Non-Jews

The Code calls for mutual respect and friendly relations between Jews and non-Jews,[38] based on mutual understanding of differences. This does not mean, of course, that the Jew is to compromise the precepts of his religion. Modern education provides for a similar attitude between religious groups based on the interchange of understanding and knowledge of customs and traditions.[39]

Jewish Attitude Towards Government

The Code insists upon loyalty to and cooperation with the government. All laws of the civil government are binding.[40] Also, one of the aims of general education is to foster such loyalty and to prepare the student for his role as a citizen.[41]

Attitude Towards Secular Studies

The attitude towards secular studies in the Shulchan Aruch is a positive one insofar as these studies help one to understand the Scriptures better.[42] In the Code, the curriculum is to consist mainly of the Bible and related texts; laws of hygiene[43] are taught as they occur in these texts. Mathematics,[44] biology,[45] grammar[46] and the other sciences are incidental to the study of the ritual in the Bible, commentaries, Talmud, and codes.

The approach in modern education differs radically from that in the Code which is concerned with training for the religious life. Modern education aims to develop the harmonious personality who understands the world around him: the world of nature, science, and humanity. The Code is not concerned with such a broad aim since its view of life is more circumscribed. However, both the Code and modern education seem to advocate the ideal that education is to train for effective living—the Code viewing effective living as being primarily in the scope of the religious life, and modern education broadening the concept to include the secular order.[47]

Educational Practices
Early Childhood Education

Home Training

In the Code, we have noted, home training education is encouraged.[48] The father is to teach the child as best he can to say the prayers and, if possible, to read. And, as we pointed out,[49] in modern education, too, it is considered "an advantage to children in learning to read, to have had experience with words and books."[50] Today, as in the past, the child's home training and pre-school learning is influenced in large measure by the demands and expectations of his environment.[51]

The Basic Curriculum

The Code advocates the study of the Torah as the basic curriculum.[52] The study of any other subject will depend on how much it is needed for the understanding of the Scriptures. Modern education, of course, advocates a varied curriculum program which will help the learner in his anticipated life experiences.[53]

Intensity of Learning

The Code urges that the pupil be occupied in his studies "the whole day and a little into the night"[54] so that he be trained to study Torah by day and by night. In modern education, as we pointed out, the aim is to direct the development of the child to the end that he may participate in his complex social environment harmoniously, for which purpose play, physical recreation, and rest are considered essential.[55] Such intensity in studying as expressed in the Code is not expected of the contemporary student by general education.

Size of Class

The Code states that the number of students in a class should not exceed twenty-five. If the class has between twenty-five and forty pupils, according to the Code, it should also have an assistant teacher. Two teachers should be appointed for a class of more than forty pupils.[56] In modern education, too, a maximum of twenty-five to thirty pupils is generally advocated.[57] Hence, we find the Code to be in consonance with another desideratum of modern practice.

Classroom Discipline

The Code advises that the teacher maintain an attitude as mild as possible, even when administering disciplinary punishment for infraction of rules.[58] In modern education, the theory is generally accepted that good results in school discipline are best obtained by "creating favorable attitudes toward desirable conduct..."[59] It would seem that the advice offered by the Code to maintain as mild a discipline as possible is in agreement with the spirit of the modern educational approach to the exercise of discipline.

The Slow Learner

Another of the educational practices advocated by the Code is patience with regard to the retarded pupil. He should be permitted to sit in with others in the hope that he may eventually make some progress in learning.[60] This is not the case in modern educational practice where special classes and curricula are provided or suggested for students of different intellectual caliber.[61] John Dewey recommends that the teaching method should be such as to avoid confusing the pupil.[62] The development of harmony in learning according to individual capacities is a basic principle in education advocated by Lull.[63] Only in a differentiated system of education can a student make better and more progress.

The Book—Tool of Learning

The Shulchan Aruch urges that the teaching materials should be free from mistakes and be attractive in appearance.[64] This practice is in agreement with that in modern education.[65] We should note here, though, that visual aids are not suggested by the Shulchan Aruch.

The Learning Process

In the process of learning, the Code advises, the student is to repeat his lesson aloud as an aid in the retention of the subject matter. The Code maintains that silent reading causes forgetting quickly the thing learned.[66] Perhaps a similar idea in modern education is the suggestion that oral rather than silent reading should be emphasized in the early stages of learning to read.[67]

The Code also advises that the student will achieve the best result in study if he understands the value of learning the Torah for its own sake, and does it willingly.[68] Dewey points out a similar idea when he remarks that the act of learning is to be a direct conscious end in itself.[69]

The Teacher[70]

Concerning the teacher, the Code is aware of the important role of the teacher in the educational process. The teacher must be morally worthy of emulation by the students. He must have a good scholastic background, and have an interest in advancing the knowledge of the Torah.[71] Similar ideas are expressed in modern education[72] where it is urged that teacher training should emphasize, among other things, an itnerest in both the pupil and the subject matter, and the importance of adequate preparation.

The teacher-pupil relation is also stressed in the Shulchan Aruch from the point of view of the teacher's influence upon the student, and, consequently, upon the latter's behavior. The relationship between the two is to be formal but friendly.[73] Modern education is also concerned with these matters. What does modern education say? Note, for instance, that "Attitudes can be shifted as a result of the selection of materials and by conscious efforts on the part of teachers."[74]

Adult Education

The Code is aware of the importance of adult education and urges continuous study and the pursuit of the knowledge of the Torah.[75] In modern education, too, adult education is stressed as a social necessity.[76]

The Education of Women[77]

In the Code, women are not expected to study the Torah per se. However, they have a responsibility to know laws pertaining to various ritual phases and practices that would help them conduct the home according to religious regulations, and bring up children to live by the teachings of the Torah. We should remember that apart from the Code, the education of Jewish women has always been regulated in accordance with the needs and demands of the time.[78]

In modern education, such a question of educating women does not exist. Each woman is free to follow her educational career as she desires.

CHAPTER IV

THE SOURCES OF JOSEPH CARO'S EDUCATIONAL IDEAS

In the foregoing chapters we have discussed Joseph Caro's life and also the basic educational principles and practices inherent in the Shulchan Aruch. We shall now proceed to discuss the main sources that might have influenced Caro.

The Main Sources

Caro in his Code often points directly to the Torah and Divine inspiration as his underlying source; and in his introduction to the Tur,[1] Caro states that he will "trace the law to the Gemara[2] (or Talmud) and its different commentators."[3] Of these commentators he singles out the RI'F,[4] the RaMBa'M,[5] and the RO'Sh.[6] In the same introduction, he also states that in case of disagreement among any of the latter three sources, or in the event a specific ruling is omitted by them, he resorts to an alternate group of scholars, namely the RaMBa'N[7] RaSHB'A,[8] Ra'N,[9] Mordecai,[10] and the SaMa'G.[11] Thus, Joseph Caro himself lists the main sources. To those we may add one more, namely the *Arba Turim* of Rabbi Jacob ben Asher. In an introduction by Caro to Jacob ben Asher's first volume of the *Arba Turim*, known as the *Tur Orach Chayim*, he states that at first he intended to append a commentary to Maimonides' *Yad Hachazakah*, the standard code, but he later changed his mind. Caro attributed this decision to the fact that Maimonides cites only one source,[12] and therefore "I would have to supply the sources of the other legal authorities, an effort that would require too much time. In order to avoid this task, I decided to append my commentary to the *Arba Turim*."[13] To this last named work Caro refers frequently either by direct quotation or by a general reference.

Actually, the form of the Shulchan Aruch itself is based on the *Arba Turim*.[14] In the same introduction, Caro enumerates further the writings of additional commentators whom he intends to consult and to use their legal decisions as an ultimate resort only. We therefore feel that these may be classified as secondary sources.[15]

We know that the correct interpretation of the Torah was a major concern of Caro's. Perplexed by the variations in interpretation and the contradictory treatises he examined, he exclaimed: "... for the Torah has become not merely two Torahs, [referring to the Written and Oral Laws] but innumerable Torahs due to the many interpretations of its laws."[16] Thus, we felt that some examples of Caro's interpretations of the Bible will, accordingly, be of interest to us. In one instance, we have the hygienic injunction against withholding bowel movement. This he presents as a transgression of the commandment: "Ye shall not make[17] yourselves abominable."[18]

From other passages in the Torah he derives ethical, ritual, or legalistic precepts:

> The Judge should be very careful not to take a bribe even to justify the one who is right, and just as the taker [of the bribe] transgresses the commandment of "Thou shalt take no gift [bribery]"[19] so too the giver is guilty of transgression of the commandment "Thou shalt not put a stumbling block[20] before the blind."[21]
>
> One who is careful to wear fringes[22] will be privileged to see the Glory.[23]
>
> Upon putting on the phylacteries[24] let one direct his thought toward the Almighty, blessed be He, who commanded us to put them on.[25]
>
> It is a positive commandment in Torah to give alms according to one's ability ... and those who close their eyes to it transgress [the commandment of] "Thou shalt not harden thy heart[26] nor close thy hand"[27]
>
> It is forbidden to steal even a thing of minute value, even by way of jest or even with the intention of returning, so that one might not accustom himself to stealing. Anyone who steals even a farthing's worth transgresses the commandment of "Thou shalt not steal"[28] and he must pay whether he stole from a Jew or a non-Jew, an adult or from a minor."[29]

Some passages in the Code indicate that an underlying source of inspiration and influence was the fact of his reverence for the Creator. Caro's piety is evidenced in many passages of his Code. We cite the following:

> One should strengthen oneself like a lion to rise in the morning to serve one's Creator.[30]
>
> Let one not say "I am well secluded in my privacy [rooms], who can see me?" For the Holy One, blessed be He, His glory fills the universe.[31]
>
> When time for [morning] prayer has come, one is forbidden to go to his neighbor's house to bid him peace [before prayer] for the name of the Almighty is Peace.[32]

> Let one tarry a while in preparation for prayer so that he direct his heart to the Almighty.[33]

We have noted at the beginning of this chapter that Maimonides, or as he is known to the Talmudic world, the Ramba'M, exerted a great influence upon Caro. In fact, Caro was so much impressed with the Ramba'M's *Yad Hachazakah*, that he wrote a commentary on it, the *Kesef Mishnah*.[34] When the *Yad*, (an abridged form of the *Yad Hachazakah*), appeared, Caro's commentary became a major feature. Caro hoped, by means of his commentary, to enhance the prestige and popularity of Maimonides' code. From this devotion and interest in Maimonides, we would judge that Caro was greatly influenced by him; and we can easily discern this influence in a comparison of the content and style[35] of a number of typical passages from Caro's Shulchan Aruch and Maimonides' *Yad Hachazakah*. We must point out, however, that while Maimonides and Caro drew upon the Talmud directly and each studied Talmudic language, the passages which we are citing generally incorporate the style and language of Maimonides' code which partially utilizes the wording of the Talmud.

We can observe some of the similarities between the code of Caro and Maimonides. When Caro cites Maimonides, he usually does so in the form of an exact quotation, and only seldom does he deviate from this practice.[36] Caro always uses Maimonides' system of numbering and paragraphing.[37] He commonly adopts the decisions of Maimonides. Additional and perhaps more concrete evidence showing that Caro was influenced in large measure by Maimonides, who combines regulations from several Talmudic tractates dealing with a given subject, may be seen from the fact that Caro quotes the law from Maimonides rather than from the original sources. Thus, the comparative passages discussed below, beginning with the words "Elementary school teachers"[38] are indexed in the Shulchan Aruch by Rabbi Moses Rivkash, as follows:

> The first statement, namely "Elementary school teachers are to be provided in every city," is taken directly from the Babylonian Talmud;[39] the second statement, namely, "And a city that has no school teachers, its citizens are to be excommunicated until such provision is made" is taken directly from the other tractate in the Babylonian Talmud;[40] the third sentence, namely, "And if they persist in their refusal [then] the city itself should be banned" is taken from Maimonides.[41]

Caro himself, in his commentary, *Kesef Mishneh*, on Maimonides' *Yad Hachazakah*, remarks that "Our Master [Maimonides] sought to keep both the Talmudic expressions 'excommunicated' and 'banned' together."[42]

We wish also to point out that the Talmud does not always use language that lends itself easily to codification. Thus, the passage beginning with the words "It is the duty of every Jew to study the Torah, be he poor or rich, healthy or ill..."[43] is a direct quotation from Maimonides. The Talmudic passage reads:

> Our Rabbis taught: the poor, the rich, the sensual [wicked] come before the [heavenly] court. They say to the poor: Why have you not occupied yourself with the Torah? Were you poorer than Hillel?... To the rich they say: ... Were you perchance richer than R. Eleazar b. Harsom?... To the sensual person they would say ...Were you perchance more beautiful than Joseph?[44]

We note from the foregoing cited passages that while Caro certainly knew of the Talmudic sources, in his code he generally followed Maimonides' version, often including his decision.

We also pointed out previously that Caro quotes copiously from the *Tur* and traces the law to its source in the Talmud, if it has its roots in it. In the opinion of this writer the *Yad Hachazakah* of Maimonides, and the *Arba Turim* of Rabenu Yaacov ben Asher, as well as the Talmud may be classified as the major sources, the *Yad Hachazakah* and the *Arba Turim* being considered the immediate sources. At this point it will be appropriate to note several excerpts which can be compared with their parallel references in the Shulchan Aruch.

Concerning education

Caro
Elementary school teachers are to be provided in every city. And a city that has no school teachers, its citizens are to be excommunicated until such provision is made. And if they persist in their refusal [then] the city itself should be banned; for the world endures only for the sake of the breath of school children.[45]

Maimonides
Elementary school teachers are to be provided in every country, in every district, and in every city. Citizens that do not engage an elementary school teacher should be excommunicated until they do so. And if they persist in this, the city itself should be banned; for the world endures only for the sake of the breath of school children.[46]

Talmud[47]
Joshua b. Gamala[48] ... ordained that teachers of your children be appointed in each district and each town.[49]

Resh Lakish[50] said in the name of R. Judah the Prince:[51] "The world endures only for the sake of the breath of school children. . . . Every town in which there are no school children shall be destroyed. Rabina[52] said: "It shall be laid desolate."[53]

Tur
Elementary school teachers are to be [appointed] in each and every city. And the citizens of any city that has no [elementary school] teacher are to be placed under a ban until they engage elementary school teachers. And if [despite the ban] they did not engage teachers, it [the city] should be destroyed, for the world endures for the sake of the breath of school children.[54]

Concerning the study of the Torah:

Caro
He needed to study and his son needed to study, and if he cannot afford to pay for both; if both are of equal [intelligence then] he has preference over his son. But if his son has better grasp and understanding [then] the son has preference over him. And even so, he himself should not cease learning.[55]

Maimonides
He wanted to study the Torah, and he has a son who needs to study the Torah. He has preference over his son. But if his son has better grasp and understanding, the son has preference over him; even so he should not cease learning.[56]

Talmud
If he has himself to teach and his son to teach, he takes precedence over his son. If his son is industrious, bright, and retentive, his son takes precedence over him.[57]

Tur
[If] he was in need of learning, and if he has a son to be taught but he can not afford [to pay] the tuition fee for both; if both are equal [in ability] he takes preference over his son; and if his son is more apt and intelligent, the son takes precedence.[58]

RA'SH
He needs to study and his son needs to study. He takes precedence over his son. . . . If his son is industrious, bright, and attentive, his son takes precedence over him and this is[59] the law.

Caro
It is the duty of every Jew to study the Torah, be he poor or rich, healthy or ill, young or old, even the poor that go from house to house, even a married man [burdened] with a family is obligated to fix a regular hour for the study of the Torah by day and by night, as it is written, "And thou[60] shalt meditate in it day and night."[61]

Maimonides

It is the duty of every Jew to study the Torah, be he poor or rich, healthy or ill in body, young or of hoary age, whose strength is spent, or even if he were [so] poor [that he is] supported by charity [earned] through begging from house to house, even if he is married and with family, it is incumbent upon him to set aside fixed time by day and by night for the study of the Torah, as it is written, "And thou shalt meditate in it[62] by day and night."[63]

Talmud

Our Rabbis taught: The poor, the rich, the sensual ["wicked"] come before the [heavenly] court. They say to the poor: Why have you not occupied yourself with the Torah? Were you poorer than Hillel?....[64] To the rich they say: ... Were you perchance richer than R. Eleazar b. Harsom?[65] ... To the sensual person they would say: ...Were you perchance more beautiful than[66] Joseph[67]?

Tur

Each and every Israelite is duty bound to study the Torah, be he poor or rich, healthy in body or suffering from aches and pain, young or of hoary age. Even the poor door beggar, even a married man with a family must set aside a fixed time to study Torah by day and night as it is written: "Thou shalt[68] meditate therein day and night."[69]

Caro

Just as one is to teach his son, one is commanded to teach his son's son, as it is written, "But make them known to thy sons' sons."[70] And not only [is he commanded to teach] his son's son but it is the duty of every educated Jew to teach students for they, too, are called children.[71]

Maimonides

Just as one is obligated to teach his son so one is commanded to teach his son's son, as it is written: "But make them known to thy sons and thy sons' sons."[72] And not only [is he commanded to teach] his son's son but it is the duty of each and every educated Jewish man to teach all the students even though they are not his sons.[73]

Talmud

Now, is the grandfather under this obligation [of teaching his grandson]?[74] Surely it was taught: *And ye shall teach them [unto] your sons ... and thou shalt make them known unto thy sons and thy sons' sons.*[75]

R. Joshua b. Levi said: He who teaches his grandson Torah, the Writ regards him as though he had received it [direct] from Mount Sinai.[76]

Tur

Just as he is commanded to teach his son, so he is obligated to train his son's son, as it is written: Thou shalt make them known unto thy sons,[77] and unto thy sons' sons. And not only [is he commanded to teach] his son's sons but it is the duty of every educated Jew to teach students, for they, too, are called children.[78]

RI'F
... And just as one is obligated to teach his son, so he is obligated to teach his son's son as it is written... R. Joshua b. Levi said: He who teaches his grandson Torah, the Writ regards him as though he had received it [direct] from Mount Sinai.[79]

Concerning the giving of alms:

Caro
One needs to give charity with a cheerful face, with happiness and wholeheartedness and commiserate with the poor man in his troubles, and speak to him always comfortingly. And if he gives alms with an angry and disgruntled face, he loses the worth of his [good] deed.[80]

Maimonides
Anyone who gives alms to the poor with a disgruntled look... even if he gave a thousand golden pieces, he loses the merit for his [good] deed; but [on the contrary] one should give alms with a cheerful countenance and commiserate with him [the poor man] on his troubles and console him.[81]

Caro
The measure of [giving] alms, if he can [afford,] let him give according to the needs of the poor. And if he cannot [afford] the amount requested then let him give one-fifth of his income which is well fulfilled the utmost requirements of the command. One-tenth is that of the middle of the scale of attributes. Less than this is that of [one with] a grudging[82] eye.[83]

Maimonides
The measure of [giving] alms, if he can afford, let him give according to the needs of the poor....[84] And if the giver cannot [afford] the amount requested, let him give as much as he can. And how much [should he give]? One-fifth of his income meets the utmost requirements of the command. One-tenth is that of an average donor. Less than this is that of one who possesses[85] a grudging eye.[86]

Talmud
... If a man wishes to spend liberally [in charity] he should not spend more than a fifth [of his wealth] ... [since by spending more] he might himself come to be in need [of the help] of people.[87]

Tur
As to the measure of giving [alms], if he can [afford], let him give according to

the needs of the poor. And if he can not [afford] the amount requested, then let him give as much as he can. And how much should he give? One-fifth of his income fulfills the utmost requirements of the command. One-tenth is that of the middle of the scale of attributes. Less than this is that of [one with] a grudging eye.[88]

Talmud

If he is a beggar who goes from door to door... we do not listen to his request for a large gift, but we do listen to his request for a small gift.[89]

R. Hiyya said to his wife: When a poor man comes, be quick to offer him bread.... R. Gamaliel Beribbi said: He who is merciful to others, mercy is shown to him by Heaven, while he who is not merciful to others, mercy is not shown to him by Heaven.[90]

Tur

One never waxes poor from giving of alms and no evil occurs to him, nor does it cause him loss, as it is written: "And the work of righteousness shall be peace."[91] And anyone that has pity on the poor, the Holy One, Blessed be He, has pity on him.[92]

Rabenu Asher, known as RA'SH

If a man wishes to spend liberally [in charity] he should not spend more than a fifth [of his wealth]... [since by spending more] he might come himself to be in need [of the help] of others.[93]

SeMa'G (*Sefer Mitzvoth Gadol*)

... We maintain, one who spends [on charity] let him not spend more than a fifth since he might come himself to be in need of others.[94]

Concerning some phases of the Sabbath:

Caro

It is permissible to hire out one's utensils to a heathen [on the eve of Sabbath] even though he uses them for work on the Sabbath, for we are not commanded that on the Sabbath utensils must be out of service.[95]

Maimonides

It is permissible to hire out utensils to a non-Jew [on the eve of Sabbath] even though he uses them for work on the Sabbath, for we are not commanded that [on the Sabbath] the utensils must be out of service.[96]

Talmud

Beth Shammai[97] maintains: Hides must not be given to a tanner nor garments to a Gentile fuller [on the eve of Sabbath] unless they can be done while it is yet day. But in all these [cases] Beth Hillel[98] permits [them].[99]

Beth Shammai maintains: A man must not lend an article to a Gentile [on the eve of Sabbath] unless he can reach his house [before sunset]: while Beth Hillel rules [unless] he can reach the house nearest the [city] wall.[100]

Tur
One may not hire out his utensils to a Gentile on the eve of Sabbath.... But he may lend them to him ... for we adhere to the rule of Beth Hillel that we are not commanded on the renting of utensils.[101]

Rabbi Nissim, known as RA'N
The law that one may hire out his utensils to a non-Jew on the eve of Sabbath, which follows the school of Hillel, was omitted by the RI'F. Apparently he follows the school of Shammai who holds that we are commanded on the resting of utensils on the Sabbath, but we do not follow this rule.[102]

Concerning suspension of the laws of the Sabbath, we compare the following:

Rabbi Isaac of Fez, known as RI'F
And the law is that ... every [case that involves a] possibility of danger to life suspends the [laws of the] Sabbath.[103]

Rabbi Nissim, known as RA'N
[And the laws of the Sabbath are rendered inoperative] even if the possibility of danger [exists] not for this Sabbath but for the next Sabbath—then it is clear that no danger to life is involved on this Sabbath, but for the next one.[104]

Mordechai (ben Hillel)
It is permissible to give one's clothes to men (to a non-Jew) towards the eve of Sabbath ... even though one knows that the non-Jew will do the work on Saturday ... for Beth Hillel permits it.[105]

Caro
Anyone who is seriously ill, it is a duty to abrogate the [commandment of the] Sabbath rest for his sake, and the more that one is alert in doing so, the more praiseworthy he is, while the one who inquires about [permission to do so] is equivalent to a murderer.[106]

When the [commandment of] Sabbath is abrogated, care should be taken that it should not be done through heathen, minors or women, but through the great [figures] of Israel and the [intellectually] mature people.[107]

Maimonides
In case of danger to life, the [commandment of] Sabbath rest, unlike any other commandment, is to be abrogated. Therefore, for the dangerously ill one should perform all that he requires on the Sabbath. When one performs these acts [on the Sabbath] one should not delegate it to strangers nor to minors, nor to servants, nor to women, in order that the Sabbath should not be taken lightly

by them. But [this work is to be performed] by the great [figures] of Israel and the sages themselves.[108]

Talmud

If one has pain in his throat, he may pour medicine into his mouth on the Sabbath, because it is a possibility of danger to human life and every danger to human life suspends the [laws of the] Sabbath.[109]

The possibility of danger to human life renders inoperative the laws of the Sabbath.... Nor are these things to be done by Gentiles or minors, but by Jewish adults ... and one need not obtain permission from the Beth Din.[110]

[A blow on] the hand or on the foot is like an internal wound, and the Sabbath may be desecrated on its account.[111]

One who was bitten by a mad dog is given to eat from the lobe of the liver ... on the Sabbath.[112]

Tur

Anyone whose illness might turn worse ... the Sabbath may be defiled for his sake. And it should not be done by minors, non-Jews or women but by Jews of high station. And the one that hastens [to help] is certainly praiseworthy. And there is no need to ask permission of the [religious] court, but the one that hastens to save a soul is [indeed] praiseworthy.[113]

CHAPTER V

THE RELATION OF THE SHULCHAN ARUCH TO LATER THEORIES AND PRACTICES OF JEWISH EDUCATION

Introductory Note

The previous chapters discussed Joseph Caro's life, the development of the Shulchan Aruch,[1] the educational principles and practices embodied in the Shulchan Aruch,[2] the basic educational principles and practices embodied in the Shulchan Aruch in relation to modern education,[3] and the sources that had direct or indirect influence upon Joseph Caro's Code.[4]

This chapter will demonstrate the extent to which the Shulchan Aruch itself has been the subject of study or an influence upon the curricula of Jewish educational institutions, both religious and secular, in various countries at different periods. In the main, our study will refer to those countries where large Jewish communities have existed. In the case of Russia, the historical background relative to Jewish education will be given in some detail, but the present-day situation can be discussed only briefly because of lack of sufficient and reliable data.[5]

The periods to be covered will differ with the countries. Thus, while the Shulchan Aruch was known in Europe during the sixteenth century to the extent that a copy of it was "found in everyone's house,"[6] in America the study of the Shulchan Aruch, even now, is in its beginnings.

Recognition of the Shulchan Aruch in the Seventeenth Century

The Status of the Shulchan Aruch in Poland and Russia[7]

In 1618, the Vaad Arba Aratzoth, or the Council of Four Lands,[8] the representative body of Great Poland,[9] Little Poland[10] Red or Polish Russia,[11] Volaynia,[12] and Lithuania,[13] ordered the use of a prayer book which was revised for correct grammatical structure according to the requirements of the Shulchan Aruch.[14]

The same committee passed a number of different ordinances concerning the Shulchan Aruch:

52

In 1663[15] the committee ordered that the newly printed copies of the Shulchan Aruch which carried the emendations by Rabbi Moses Isserles,[16] the Polish Talmudic scholar, and the sources for each law indicated by Rabbi Mosheh Rivkas,[17] Russian Talmudist, should not be reprinted without permission of Rabbi Rivkas.

In the year 1670 the committee announced "a certain amount of money partly as a gift and partly as a loan, for the purpose of printing the [third part of the] Shulchan Aruch, [the] *Eben Haezer*. . . .[18]

In 1689 the same committee forbade the reprinting of the first part of the Shulchan Aruch, the *Orach Chayim*, for ten years without the permission of the editor, Rabbi Judah Leib of Pinsk, a Russian Talmudist.[19]

The committee was eager to assist in the publication of a brochure about the Shulchan Aruch "whose codified law we follow."[20]

The foregoing references indicate the important role the Shulchan Aruch played as the authoritative code among Polish, Russian, and Lithuanian Jewry. To these we may add the statement by Rabenu Israel Meyir Ha-Cohen, known as the Chofetz Chayyim, 1837–1933, in his introduction to the Shulchan Aruch.[21] He held that the Shulchan Aruch-Orach Chayim is a daily necessity for every Jew every day of the year, in order to fulfill the Commandments of the Torah; without it no Jew may lift a hand or foot. This is what the Torah means when it tells us: "Yo shall therefore keep my statutes, and my judgments which if a man do, he shall live by them. . . .[22] And so Caro prepared for us his pure Shulchan [Aruch] or the prepared table that we may know practical laws."[23] An equally important statement is made by Rabbi Moses Isserles in his introduction to the Shulchan Aruch-Choshen Mishpat,[24] to the effect that Joseph Caro prepared for us the Shulchan Aruch, leaving no room for adverse criticism except to point out the customs in these countries (Poland, Russia, Germany, France, among others), "And I consider his words in the Shulchan Aruch as if they were given by the Almighty through Moses."[25] Again, Sversky, in his introduction to Joseph Caro's *Maggid Maysharim*,[26] says that the Shulchan Aruch is the most reliable and the most widespread code after the Talmud, and that every religious Jew should direct his actions in accordance with the rules presented in the Shulchan Aruch. To this we may also add statements by secular authorities in Jewish history such as S.M. Dubnow, that by the middle of the seventeenth century "the authority of the Shulchan Aruch as emended by Isserles had been so firmly established in Poland that this code was studied and expounded with even greater zeal than the Talmud."[27] And we may also add the statement by Graetz that the Shulchan Aruch soon became the "infallible standard authority through the East, in Italy and even in Poland."[28]

We have thus pointed out the authoritative status of the code in Poland and Russia, and will now proceed to illustrate further the importance of the code as a subject of study in religious educational institutions.

The Shulchan Aruch as a Subject of Study[29]

When Joseph Caro published the first edition of the Shulchan Aruch, he divided its contents into thirty daily lessons "so that each and every Jew might learn each day one part, with the result that each month he will repeat the study."[30] We have pointed out in the preceding paragraphs that the Shulchan Aruch has been, generally, an integral part of the Jewish study curriculum, and shall now discuss the matter in more detail.

It may be remarked at this point that until the beginning of the Haskalah or Enlightenment Movement, about the end of the eighteenth century, the primary aim of Jewish education in Poland and Russia[31] was to inculcate in the Jewish child reverence for God and the desire to fulfill His Commandments even to the point of self-sacrifice.[32]

Rabbi Nathan Nata Hanover, Russian Talmudist, tells us that the Jews in Poland had a high educational standard, for "there was hardly a Jewish house where Torah would not be studied; either the head of the family himself was a scholar, or his son, or son-in-law, or he would have at his table a Talmudic student."[33]

From an answer of Rabbi Chayyim of Chanz, Poland, to Rabbi David Dayitch of Yarmut, Hungary, we read that in Poland everyone "busies himself day and night in the study of the Torah, in the understanding of the laws of the Talmud, and the Shulchan Aruch...."[34]

Another seventeenth-century writer, Rabbi Zelig ben R. Itzchak Isaac of Polotzk, Russia, says: "When the father notices that his son is not given to study, let him teach his son the Bible, the prophets, Hagiographa, followed by Mishnah and the Shulchan Aruch."[35]

Rabbi Pinchas ben R. Yehudah[36] advises his son similarly to follow a curriculum that will fit one to be active in teaching. After listing several subjects, he remarks: "And for this I can vouch, that if you learn the Shulchan Aruch, your grasp will become so sharp that you will know at a glance the latest decisions."[37]

We have in addition to the foregoing, the testimony of the student in the reminiscences of Rabbi Yehuda Yudel[38] who describes his joy when as a young man he began to learn and to understand this Code and its interpreters.

Asaf,[39] quoting from *Orchoth Chayyim* by R. Chayim of Volhozin,[40] informs us that the curriculum in Poland consisted of at least three folios of the Talmud daily and then the Shulchan Aruch, until the student becomes expert in it [and knows it] by heart."

So concerned were some rabbis that their descendants should perpetuate the learning and practices of the Code that they left statements in their wills to this effect. Thus, Rabbi Sheftel, one-time Chief Rabbi of Posen,[41] in his will, urges his children to include in their curriculum of study, indispensable to anyone "who wants to spread the Torah among Israel," always to "review the

Shulchan Aruch so that you would know it by heart as you know the Psalm 'Ashrey,' so that you can expertly find the law you need."[42] And Rabbi Ya'acov of Lisa in a similar will, advises his children to follow a curriculum which will include, among other subjects, "a page of the Talmud or of the Shulchan Aruch-Orach Chayim."[43]

A plaintive note reaches us from Rabbi Yosef ben Meir (b. 1727-d. 1793) of Lwów,[44] Poland, concerning the manner which students preferred to study the Shulchan Aruch. He notes that some students studied the Code only superficially, with the shortest commentary.

> And the part of Orach Chayim they do not want to learn at all saying that the books on ethics are good for preachers only. Only the laws pertaining to Passover they would learn, for it is a must, like the Yoreh Deah. But I say that it is forbidden to utter such a statement, for I wish we studied every day a lesson in ethics for "the beginning of wisdom is the fear of the Almighty."And the compiler [of the Shulchan Aruch] was a God-fearing man. Such laws as the one concerning the washing of the hands, and the like, represent deep thought in the Mishnah and in legalistic literature; and a short-cut to these laws leaves out the quintessence. Therefore I say that it is necessary that one should study all four parts of the Shulchan Aruch with all the commentaries. Only then can one grasp fully the imminence of the Law. And all the laws in the part Orach Chayim are awe-inspiring and represent a search into the truth.[45]

In our discussion of the status and prestige of the Shulchan Aruch in Russia and Poland, we observed that the Code was recognized by the Council of Four Lands, the representative body of the four provinces in Russia and Poland. Outstanding rabbis recommended that the Shulchan Aruch should be a vital part of the study of the rabbinical student[46] as well as that of the layman. We shall now proceed to examine the status of the Shulchan Aruch in other Jewish communities.

The Status of the Shulchan Aruch in Some European Countries

In 1640,[47] Rabbi Shabbathay Meshorer Bas noted that in the Talmud Torah, i.e., Jewish communal school of the congregation of Amsterdam, the children of the fifth grade are taught Jewish law. "And before each holiday all students study in the Shulchan Aruch the laws pertaining to it." In the first year the pupils at this school learned to read the prayer book. In the second year they studied the Pentateuch in Hebrew. In the third year translation of the Pentateuch into the vernacular[48] was emphasized, also the commentary of Rashi. During the fourth year they studied the prophets and the Hagiographa. In the fifth year they studied Hallachah and grammar. Before each holiday they studied the pertinent rules in the Shulchan Aruch. In the sixth and final year they continued the study of the law and the codes of Maimonides, the Tur, and the Beth Yoseph, among other writings.[49]

It would seem proper to note here that the Jews in their personal conduct governed themselves according to the Talmudic-rabbinic law. This law which was accepted by all Jews was codified several times before it arrived at its most definitive and popular form in the Shulchan Aruch.[50]

Rabbi Yehuda ben Bezalel of Prague, also known as the "great Rabbi Loew," who lived during the sixteenth century, related[51] the following points of interest:

> The ancient Jews maintained and preserved their Torah in the face of oppression and persecution, but we sit calmly and complacently in our homes, and if we are faced with a problem of law or a question of religion, we use the aid of the Prepared Table [Shulchan Aruch] of which people say, "This is the Table that is before the Lord" [Ezekiel 41:22]. At this table the great and the small gather. . . . They all seek to take their spiritual food from this "great table" without attempting to delve into the reasons and the purposes that lie behind the precepts set before them upon this table.

We note here that the Shulchan Aruch was viewed as an obstacle to the study of the Mishnah and the Talmud.

From a will left by Rabbi Mosheh Hasid of Prag (17th century in Bohemia) we learn that "in the Shulchan Aruch you should see to it that you should review the laws [and] the paragraphs inside and by heart."[52]

A similar will was left by Rabbi Yonah Landsofar (1678–1712) to his children. He advises them to give most of their time of study to the Shulchan Aruch—"And even the one that is not learned . . . should listen to lectures on the Shulchan Aruch."[53]

One of the earliest indications of the status of the Shulchan Aruch in Italy comes from Samuel ben Nehemias,[54] who informs us that in the Talmud Torah the curriculum of the fourth grade included instruction in the Code.[55] Three schools began teaching the Code in the second grade, namely, a Talmud Torah at Modena (1597 and 1679);[56] one at Verona (1688 and later 1759);[57] and another at Ferrara 1767).[58] We have information of a similar nature from a copy of regulations concerning the curriculum of the Talmud Torah at Padua of the year 1715,[59] where in the third grade the teacher was to initiate the study of the Code, to be dealt with every Wednesday morning after breakfast, as an extra-curricular activity.

The teaching of the Shulchan Aruch in Germany in the eighteenth century is described by Itzchak Wetzler.[60] He advises that the curriculum for nonacademic courses should include the Shulchan Aruch-Orach Chayim (first part), while for the curriculum of the potential scholar, the entire Shulchan Aruch (all four parts) should be taught.

We note also, from a letter written by David Friedlander dated march 30, 1799[61] that while Jewish education was at a low ebb, yet the study of the Shulchan Aruch was advised, along with the Pentateuch, as a bare minimum without which a Jewish boy was considered an ignoramus.

Rabbi Chaim Yair Bachrach (1609–1702) of Germany, in one of his responsa, complains of the lack of interest in Jewish studies among German Jews. He recommends that the study of the Jew who wishes to follow the commandments of the Torah in daily life, should include among other subjects the Shulchan Aruch-Orach Chayim and Yoreh Deah. "This fulfills the requirements of the sages."[62]

Rabbi Itzchak ben R. Avraham Molcho of Turkey, tells us that when a poor student began to buy books and longed to acquire works on legal subjects, he would say, "When I will have money I will buy a Shulchan Aruch...."[63]

The Study of the Shulchan Aruch from the Eighteenth Century On

Introductory Note

We have discussed in the previous pages the status of the Shulchan Aruch and the extent to which it was studied in several countries through the seventeenth century, for the most part.

In the discussion which follows, we shall trace the study of this Code from the eighteenth century to the present time. We thus hope to demonstrate further the importance of the Shulchan Aruch in Jewish religious life.[64]

Poland

Daniel Neufeld (1814–1874), an outstanding authority[65] on Jewish education in Poland, proposed that the local government should establish special schools for Jewish students, so that they would not have to attend school on the Sabbath. He felt that the program of study in these schools include, among other Jewish subjects, the study of the first part of the Shulchan Aruch, the Orach Chayim.[66] This proposal is another indication of the important role the study of the Shulchan Aruch played in Jewish religious life in his generation.

The orthodox Mizrachi schools, which represented a national-religious ideology, were organized in 1927,[67] under a central body known as "Yavneh." They operated a government-accredited secular program in addition to a program of religious institutions comprising over twenty-two hours of study per week.[68] In all these schools dinim,[69] or codified laws, were taught in various degrees.[70]

In 1933, the Beth Yosef Yeshivoth, a netwrok of orthodox schools, adopted during one of its meetings in Bialystok, a regulation that in all its branches[71] the Shulchan Aruch should be taught. The regulation provided specifically that "It is incumbent upon each student to study some sections of the Shulchan Aruch Orach Chayim every day."[72] However, the Beth Yosef Yeshivoth did not stress the study of the Code as did other yeshivoth where the basic curriculum centered around "the dry study of Talmud and the Shulchan Aruch."[73]

The Agudath Israel, an orthodox Jewish organization established in 1912, conducted a large number of schools. Morenu Yaacov Rosenheim, one of the leaders of the organization, demanded that the program of study include Dinim and Posekim,[74] laws and codes respectively,[75] in all its educational institutions,[76] in each according to its level.

In 1929 the Agudath Israel established a network of schools: the Chorev schools for boys, and the Beth Yaacov schools for girls. The Chorev schools carried a program which combined secular and religious studies, the latter consisting of "prayers, the Bible and commentaries, Mishnah, Gemorah and Dinim" which is defined parenthetically as ("a prescribed code of behavior in conformity with the Talmud").[77]

The Beth Yaacov schools for girls in Warsaw adopted (1931)[78] a program of study aimed at inculcating the basic concepts of Jewish life promulgated in the Tanach (Bible). To accomplish this aim, it was deemed necessary to add also the study of the Shulchan Aruch. The program of study was graded and calculated on a monthly basis.[79]

The following syllabus gives the monthly schedule for Grade 1:

1. ELUL (August-September)
For this month which directly precedes the Jewish New Year and the Day of Atonement, the following laws were studied: Teshuvah (repentance); Rosh Hashanah (New Year); the Blowing of the Shofar (Ram's Horn); and of Selichoth (Supplications).[80]

2. TISHRI (September-October)
Here the subject matter dealt with those laws concerning behavior toward others: honor to parents; blessings; those concerning Yom Kippur (Day of Atonement) and the meal before it; and the laws concerning Succoth (The Festival of Tabernacles).[81]

3. CHESHVAN (October-November)
During this period the study of the rules concerning the morning ritual of washing the hands and those of the various blessings over foods and drinks was required.

4. KISLEV (November-December)
At this time further rules concerning honor for parents were studied as were the laws concerning Chanukah (Feast of Lights). Then followed a review of laws studied previously.

5. TEVETH (December-January)

Here the laws of the Fast Day of Assarah BeTeveth were studied together with those of other fast days occurring during the year. Some of the Sabbath laws were also considered.[82]

6. SHEVATH (January-February)

During this month the blessings concerning "Asher Yatzar," said upon washing the hands after leaving the toilet; "Hamavdil," a prayer reminding one of the difference between Sabbath and other days of the week; the answering of "Amen" after hearing a blessing; and the rules concerning Tu Beshevat, celebrating the New Year of the Trees (Arbor Day)[83] were dealt with.

7. ADAR (February-March)

Here the laws concerning the festival of Purim (Feast of Lots), and of sending gifts to friends during this festival were studied. Besides discussing the rules concerning preparation for Sabbath,[84] it was suggested that the teacher deal with the deeds of various sages as part of this preparation. Topics concerning the obligations one has to the Almighty were also proposed for consideration.[85]

8. NISAN (March-April)

In this section, the laws concerning the Festival of Passover and the Passover night meal were studied.[86] Discussions concerning the Diaspora and the redemption from Egypt were also germane.

9. IYAR (April-May)

At this time some of the laws of "Muktzeh," concerning articles forbidden to be carried on Sabbath were studied, along with those concerning table manners.[87] Next, the rules about Lag Baomer (the spring harvest festival) together with the story of Rabbi Akiba and his disciples were discussed.[88]

10. SIVAN (May-June)

Here the laws concerning Shavuoth or the Feast of Weeks were studied along with the laws of kindling the lights of Sabbath eve, and those dealing with honor for parents. Discussions on the Ten Commandments, and on those laws pertaining to Sabbath meals were also carried on.[89]

The program of study for Grade 2 had basically the same format but was greater in depth. Additional laws not studied hitherto were included. Thus, Grade 2 had, additionally, the following topics of study from the Shulchan Aruch.[90]

For the month of Elul, the New Year was treated as the Day of Judgment and New Year blessings as well as the special blessing uttered on many new occasions, *Shehecheyanu*, were learned.[91]

On Tishri the teacher taught the rituals pertaining to the fast of the

Day of Atonement, the Havdalah [a prayer differentiating between the Day of Atonement and the other Days], and that of Simchath Torah [the Feast of Rejoicing of the Law].

For Cheshvan, the reading of the Law on Sabbath; a discussion of the written and the oral law, and of Hillel and his attitude toward proselytes was required.[92]

In Kislev the additional studies of Grade 2 were those relating to the blessings uttered upon the occurrence of thunder and lightning, and on observing the rainbow; plus a discussion on the importance of Adam, the first man.[93]

The agenda on Teveth included topics on the land of Israel, the Temple and Jerusalem, the destruction of the Temple, vengeance and bearing a grudge.[94] The latter was in connection with the story of Kamtza and Bar Kamtza, whose feud was said to have contributed to the destruction of Jerusalem.[95]

During Shevat the subject matter included the story of "Rabbi" [Rabbi Judah the Prince][96] and the benedictions repeated over the cup of wine.

For Adar the laws on matzah [the unleavened bread] and those concerning the eating of fish and meat, soup on Sabbath were studied.[97]

On Nisan the laws and discussions concerning Passover were again in the fore.

The Manna given in the desert was discussed in some detail in Iyar, and a review was made of various blessings and laws concerning foods.

During the month of Sivan the laws of Sabbath were studied in relation to Leviticus XIX, 3, "Ye shall fear, every man, his mother and his father, and my Sabbaths shall ye keep."[98]

The period of study for Grade 3 was enlarged further. The Kitzur Shulchan Aruch was studied with reference to laws concerning holidays.[99] It was also part of the program of study of Grades 4 to 8 inclusive, it being suggested that for Grade 8 the study of the Code be increased from two hours weekly to three hours, if possible.[100]

The yeshivah in Warsaw known as the Mesivtah, also an orthodox institution of high Talmudic learning, was founded in 1919. It was administered by a group of prominent orthodox rabbis headed by Rabbi Meir Don Polatzky.[101] The yeshivah had a five-year curriculum which prescribed instruction in the Shulchan Aruch, among other subjects. The student was required to cover the Orach Chayim, the first part of Yoreh Deah, and parts of Choshen Mishpat.[102]

The Yeshivah Kether Torah of Radomsk, Poland, was founded in 1926 by

Rabbi Shelomo Chanoch HaCohen Rabinowitz.[103] It was founded for the specific purpose of "studying Torah for its own sake,"[104] and to produce scholars in Talmud and in rabbinic literature rather than professional rabbis. This yeshivah was one of thirty-three yeshivoth by the same name spread over Poland.[105] The Shulchan Aruch-Yoreh Deah and Choshen Mishpat, subjects usually required of candidates for the rabbinate, were not included in the program.[106] This writer would assume that the Shulchan Aruch-Orach Chayim was taught because it contains rules and laws pertaining to everyday life.

In Poland there were many intimate synagogues conducted by small, closely-knit groups, known by the Yiddish term *shtiblach*[107] [rooms]. These *shtiblach* were synagogues in which young people and adults studied informally. In some of the large *shtiblach* the number of students reached two or three hundred.[108] Since the purpose of the study was, in the main, to prepare the student for applying the laws of the Torah to daily life, the study of the Shulchan Aruch and its various dinim was considered as important as the study of the Talmud.[109] The study was self-imposed, in accordance with the first rule of the Shulchan Aruch-Orach Chayim which reads: "...Be strong as a lion" to fulfill the will of the Almighty. The study began at five o'clock in the morning and continued until seven.[110] Between seven and eight A.M. morning prayers were conducted.[111] After this the students went home for breakfast. Some returned for study for a full day; others such as artisans and business men, came to spend their leisure time. Thus we have an instance where the Shulchan Aruch was studied by large groups of adults for its own sake.

The Tarbuth schools in Poland were nationalistic and secular rather than religious, aimed at giving students a well rounded education. They began to appear toward the end of the nineteenth century in Europe.[112] By 1917, the program of study centered around Jewish cultural and Jewish national aspects, and included the study of *possekim*[113] or legalistic literature, of which the Shulchan Aruch is a part. However, the program of study in these schools in 1933 showed that this area of study had been eliminated.[114]

The Institute for Jewish studies and research in Warsaw, Poland, founded in 1928, was presided over by Doctor Mordechai Braude, a senator,[115] in the Warsaw SEYM. In 1929-1930 a department for rabbinics was established. The program of study covered a period of four years,[116] and included lectures on theShulchan Aruch-Yoreh Deah.[117] Among the subjects listed for the final examination was the Shulchan Aruch.[118]

The rabbinical seminary Tachkemoni, maintained by the Mizrachi organization, was established in Warsaw in 1920. Rabbi Moshe Soloveiczyk was one of its most outstanding leaders.[119] The seminary had a five-year program in which the study of the Shulchan Aruch was offered as a basic subject.[120] In the final two grades, the Shulchan Aruch-Yoreh Deah was stressed.[121]

In 1958, ten small schools of the Talmud Torah type were reported in

Poland.[122] In 1959, seventeen such schools were known to be operating.[123] No other information is available in this area, and we may perhaps assume that the Shulchan Aruch is taught in some measure in these schools.

Rumania-Bessarabia

In Kishenev, Bessarabia, a yeshivah was founded in 1860. The program of study at the time included the Talmud and Posekim, which of course implies the study of the Shulchan Aruch, among other codes. In 1908 the name of the yeshivah was changed to Yeshivah Zibburith al Shem Perlmutter-Kligman.[124] In the same year the yeshivah decided to grant the title of rabbi to its graduates. Beginning with the third grade in this institution, systematic study of Posekim was begun. The Shulchan Aruch Yoreh Deah was studied in conjunction with other Posekim. In the fourth grade the second part of Yoreh Deah was completed, and the Orach Chayim and Eben Haezer were taken up. This yeshivah was closed in 1940, when Kishenev fell to the Communists.[125]

Toward the end of the nineteenth century, the Cheder Methukan, or the Modern Cheder, was established alongside the old type of cheder. The program of this new cheder was based on four to eight years of study, depending upon the students' preparation. The Kitzur Shulchan Aruch was included in the program of study.[126] In some orthodox Hebrew schools, such as the Gymnasium Mogen-David established in 1921 by the Agudath Israel, directed by Rabbi I.L. Izirelson, the Talmud and legalistic literature were included in the program of study.[127]

In 1958, the Jewish community of Rumania was supporting five hundred synagogues, a seminary in Arad, and a great number of Talmud Torahs.[128]

Hungary

Special emphasis was laid on the teaching of the Shulchan Aruch in the yeshivoth of Greater Hungary.[129] About two hundred yeshivoth existed there between 1914 and 1944. The program of study offered by the Yeshivoth Haramah in Tashnad, Transylvania, which was conducted under the directorship of Rabbi Mordechai Brisk, is offered as an example.[130] The Rosh Yeshivah or dean himself would study the Shulchan Aruch Orach Chayim every weekday after the morning prayers. On the eve of Sabbath and on Sunday, he would teach the laws from the Shulchan Aruch dealing with the Sabbath, and the first part of the Yoreh Deah.[131] On the Sabbath afternoon and again at night, he would examine the students on their mastery of the rules concerning the Sabbath in the Shulchan Aruch Orach Chayim. On Sunday, he would examine the students on the Shulchan Aruch Yoreh Deah.[132] The study of the Shulchan Aruch Orach Chayim, and the first part of Yoreh Deah as well as some of the Choshen Mishpat, was usually stressed in the other yeshivoth.[133]

The final examinations included questions on about thirty subjects included in the Shulchan Aruch Yoreh Deah and pertinent Talmudic tractates.[134]

A candidate was admitted to ordination after he had mastered the first part of the Shulchan Aruch Yoreh Deah, which contained the laws pertaining to Mikvah [ritual bath]; the laws pertaining to niddah [menstruation]; those pertaining to Passover; and pertinent Talmudic tractates, including commercial laws.[135] These laws were regarded as essential knowledge for the rabbi as the religious guide of the community.

The teaching of the Shulchan Aruch was also pursued in the Yeshivah Chatham Sofer[136] of Pressburg, Hungary. This yeshivah was founded by Rabbi Mosheh Sofer. Rabbi Sofer stated (1826) in answer to the governor's inquiry, concerning the contents of the curriculum, that the Code was taught in addition to other legalistic literature.

On Sundays, holidays, and Tuesdays, between the prayers of Minchah and Maariv, the rabbi lectured on the Shulchan Aruch.[137] In 1840, after the death of Rabbi Mosheh Sofer, his son, Shemuel Abraham Benyamin Sofer, known as the "Ketav Sofer," succeeded him as the spiritual leader. Every day, towards evening, he lectured in the yeshivah on the Shulchan Aruch Yoreh Deah, "... so as to accustom his listeners in passing legal decisions."[138] After his death in 1872, his son, Rabbi Simcha Bunim Sofer, known as the "Shevet Sofer," became the head of the Yeshivah. He instituted further improvements in the teaching of the Shulchan Aruch by inviting prominent lecturers and authorities on the Yoreh Deah.[139] After his death in 1907, his son, Rabbi Akiba Sofer, succeeded him. Many of this rabbi's students knew by heart large portions of the Shulchan Aruch Yoreh Deah.[140] This school lasted until 1940, when Rabbi Akiba Sofer left for Palestine to transplant the yeshivah there.[141]

In Budapest, in 1958, there were two Jewish secondary schools with an enrollment of two hundred Orthodox boys and girls, and a yeshivah with twelve students.[142] Even under such difficult conditions as now exist, it may be assumed that the contents of the Shulchan Aruch are taught.[143]

The yeshivah Torah VaAvodah of Hlohovic (known as *Galgoe* in Hungarian, or *Preistadt* in German) was founded in 1937. From a letter by the Rosh HaYeshivah, Rabbi A. Shwartz, dated January 28, 1938, we note that the Magen Avraham, a famous commentary on the Shulchan Aruch, was studied daily.[144] It would follow then that knowledge of the Shulchan Aruch was expected of the students in this yeshivah.[145]

Germany

In the 124 elementary Hebrew day schools that operated in Germany from 1926,[146] the program of study in the first two grades included reading, writing, benedictions, prayers, and Bible stories. In the third grade, Mishnah and Dinim were added, which implies that the Shulchan Aruch was taught. This program was then pursued on a more advanced level, until the ninth grade.[147]

The German-Jewish orthodox religious communities were interested in the Shulchan Aruch, as were Jewish religious communities the world over. Eliahu

Morpurgo, a learned Italian Jew proposed in 1786[148] that the German Jews revise the program of study in their schools and modernize it, as had been done in Italy. Specifically, he advocated that until the age of six, the child should be taught by a woman teacher, "as is the case with the Spanish and Italian Jews."[149] He further proposed that boys should begin their schoolwork before the age of three. During the first three years, reading should be emphasized. Between the ages of six to nine, the child should study Hebrew and the vernacular, along with the Pentateuch, fundamentals of grammar, Dinim, and ethics, for four hours daily—two hours in the morning and two hours in the afternoon. At the age of nine, the youth should study the Torah and translation, grammar, and the laws pertaining to Sabbath and the holidays. One hour daily should be allowed for writing Hebrew and the language of the land. During the following four years, that is, from the age of nine to thirteen, the laws in Orach Chayim and Yoreh Deah as well as ethics should be studied.[150]

Soon, leading German Jewish educators decided to modernize the Talmud Torah or community school of Berlin, established in 1819. This modern school was to add a school for secondary and one for higher education, from where "workers, businessmen, artisans and teachers, rabbis and medical doctors" were to graduate. The program of study was to include, among other subjects, the study of the Talmud and the Shulchan Aruch.[151]

Various attempts were made to establish modern Jewish orthodox religious institutions[152] that would emphasize religious subjects within a curriculum combining also secular learning. It was Rabbi Shimshon Raphael Hirsch (1808–1888), Rabbi of the Jewish Orthodox community of Frankfort-on-the-Main, who succeeded in achieving a satisfactory program of study.[153] The school, established in Frankfort in 1853, developed a nine-year program of study. From the fifth year on, the study of the Mishnah, the Talmud, and the Shulchan Aruch was introduced for qualified students.[154]

Other schools followed the program of study prepared by Rabbi Hirsch. Among these were the following: a school in Altona, established in 1839 by Rabbi I. Etlinger, the teacher of Rabbi Hirsch;[155] one in Mainz (Magenza), begun in 1859 and headed by Rabbi Lehman;[156] another established by Rabbi Z.B. Bamberger in Würzberg in 1855;[157] and that founded in 1862 in Fürth, under the guidance of Dr. Zelig Auerbach.[158]

There were also schools of higher learning of which the Talmud Unterrichtsanstalt, the Talmudical Seminary of Berlin, dating from 1852, is an example.[159] The program of study in these schools included the Tanach (Old Testament), the Mishnah, the Talmud, the Shulchan Aruch, Yiddish composition, Biblical history, and translation of prayers.[160]

In 1873 Rabbi Azriel Hildescheimer (1820–1899) established a rabbinical seminary in Berlin, with the purpose of educating orthodox rabbis.[161] The program of study included, among other subjects, the Shulchan Aruch Orach

Chayim, Yoreh Deah, and Even Haezer. The major portion of the Code was covered during the last three years.[162]

By 1890, the late Rabbi Shelomo Breuer succeeded in establishing a yeshivah in Frankfort-on-the-Main. There lectures on the Shulchan Aruch Yoreh Deah were delivered by Yaacov Pozen.[163]

In 1872, the Jewish Theological Seminary of Berlin was established with the aim of training modern rabbis, that is, those whose education includes secular subjects. The curriculum included Posekim among other religious subjects.[164]

In Posen, at the beginning of the nineteenth century, the cheder was popular.[165] The study of the Siddur or prayer book was part of the religious program, which entailed the study of the pertinent laws in the Shulchan Aruch. Boys who continued after the age of nine, studied the Shulchan Aruch, among other religious subjects.[166]

In 1920 Rabbi Mosheh Shneider established a yeshivah in Frankfort-on-the-Main, and in 1924 Rabbi Yaacov Hoffman founded another one there.[167] Between 1920 and 1930 several other yeshivoth were successfully established in different cities of Germany, such as in Nuremberg, Hamburg, Karlsbach, Leipzig, and Breslau. The program of study of these schools extended over a five-year period.[168] The program of study in 1920 shows the ground covered in the Shulchan Aruch in each grade. In the first year the Shulchan Aruch Yoreh Deah, sections 69–78[169] and 91–104[170] were taught, together with the related Talmudic tractates.[171] In the second grade, the sections of the Shulchan Aruch Orach Chayim 242–263[172] were studied. In the third grade the Shulchan Aruch Orach Chayim, sections 581–624[173] were dealt with, and also Yoreh Deah, Sections 82–86.[174] In the fifth grade the entire Kitzur Shulchan Aruch was the subject of study.[175]

A similar program of study was followed in the Jewish community high schools founded by the Agudath Israel.[176] In 1938, when Jewish students were excluded from the public schools, Jewish studies in the Jewish day schools were intensified.[177]

From the foregoing evidence, it seems clear that the study of the Shulchan Aruch in Germany, within orthodox religious Jewry, was an important phase of Jewish education.

England

According to H. Lewis, London in 1938 had several types of Jewish schools, of which the Talmud Torah had the most intensive program of religious studies.[178] He states: "It offers a smattering of that wonderful compendium of Jewish living, the Shulchan Aruch."[179]

The Jews' College in London, an institution for training rabbis, founded in 1856, records in its bulletin that an entrance examination on the Shulchan Aruch is required even of the highest ranking candidate.[180]

The program of study in the Jews' College for 1958–1959 shows the teaching of the following subjects in the Shulchan Aruch:

a) Tzitzith[181] [fringes].
b) Tefilin [phylacteries].
c) Berachoth [blessings].
d) Keriath Shema [sanctification of the Name].
e) Netilath Yadayim [washing of hands].
f) Birchath Hamazon [grace].
g) Laws of ninth of Ab [a fast day commemorating the destruction of the Temple].
h) Laws of Passover.
i) Laws of Rosh Hashonah [New Year].
j) Laws pertaining to Melicha [salting of meat].[182]
k) Tevilath Kelim [ritual submersion of dishes].
l) Milah [circumcision].
m) Pidyon-Haben [redemption of the first-born son].
n) Challah [the Sabbath bread].
o) Aveluth [laws of morning].

The school class of the Jews' College includes in its program of study selected portions of the Shulchan Aruch Yoreh Deah and Even Haezer, and the respective Talmudic tractates.[183]

The program of study for the Hazanuth or Cantoral division includes the study of selected portions from the Kitzur Shulchan Aruch, whereas the program of study for rabbinical candidates includes a knowledge of all four parts of the Shulchan Aruch, namely, the Orach Chayim, the Yoreh Deah, the Even Haezer, and the Choshen Mishpat.[184]

The Institute for the training of teachers, under the auspices of the Jews' College, requires the study of the Shulchan Aruch Orach Chayim for those teachers who intend to teach Hebrew and religion.[185] The Code is taught one hour per week.

The Jews' College is the center of Jewish orthodox education in England. However, after 1881, with the influx of Jewish refugees from Russia, Talmud Torahs and synagogue classes sprang up in several areas to satisfy the educational needs of these refugees.[186] In 1905 a Talmud Torah Trust was created with the stimulus of a fund established by Sr. Samuel Montague. In 1939 it embraced nineteen institutions.[187]

In 1941 a formal Union of Hebrew and Religion Classes was founded with 57 affiliates. The Jewish Religious Education Board had for its primary object to provide instruction in Hebrew and religion to children attending elementary public schools in the London area.

In Liverpool, a city with a Jewish population of 7,500, a Talmudical college was established.

In Leeds, where the Jewish population numbers about 25,000, a yeshivah and a Hebrew congregational school was established.

Higher studies in Jewish literature and religion were lacking in England in 1940.[188] There were, however, lectureships in rabbinics at Cambridge and at Oxford.[189]

The schools under the supervision of the Association for Promoting Torah Education in London teach the Shulchan Aruch for half an hour a week out of a total of seven hours in Jewish instruction. This is supplemented by verbal instruction in Dinim, and by the use of booklets for the various festivals which also contain most of the relevant Dinim.[190]

The Shulchan Aruch is taught directly from the original to an adult education group. At least one out of five tuition hours per week is devoted to the study of the Code itself.[191]

Israel

The program of study for the governmental elementary public schools in Israel was prepared during a period of eight years (1948–1955) and is based on the Bible, on tradition, on programs of outstanding Jewish schools in the Diaspora such as the Mizrachi schools, on the Cheder Methukan or modern private school, on Tarbuth schools whose program tends to emphasize the social-secular, and on schools of the working classes.[192]

In 1953, the Israeli government set up a unified system of education. In the program of study for the public schools and the governmental religious schools[193] of 1957 known as the Beth Sefar Hayyessodee, the study of the Shulchan Aruch is included. In the fourth grade the Kitzur Shulchan Aruch proper is used. The pupils study from specially prepared brochures entitled *Pirkei Dinim*.[194] Laws pertaining to the festival of Chanukah are studied from the Kitzur Shulchan Aruch, while those pertaining to Passover are read from a specially prepared booklet.[195] The teacher in the religious school is advised to use the text only in preparing the lessons for the earlier grades, the instruction to be done orally.[196]

Morocco

From Casablanca, Morocco, it is reported that the schools sponsored by the Ozar Hatorah organization teach the Kitzur Shulchan Aruch from the first to the eighth grades. The following time schedule is reported for each grade: In the first grade the subject is taught for 90 minutes weekly. In the second, third, and fourth grades, 120 minutes weekly are devoted to each. In the fifth, sixth, and seventh grades 90 minutes weekly are devoted to each. In the eighth grade the Kitzur Shulchan Aruch is taught for 135 minutes weekly.

In the yeshivoth, the Shulchan Aruch Mishnah Berurah[197] is taught for one hour daily. There is also a school which specializes in teaching Shechitah (ritual slaughtering) and in which the Shulchan Aruch Yoreh Deah is taught during the entire day.[198]

Canada

The Jewish population in Canada was estimated in 1950 to be approximately 200,000.[199] In some Jewish schools the Shulchan Aruch is taught. The text used, however, is that by Israel Konowitz. The Young Israel school in Montreal begins using the text in grade five. The United Talmud Torahs employ it in their high school classes. In the lower classes, the teacher discusses the Dinim orally. The emphasis, however, is on Biblical studies.[200]

Montreal has the largest Jewish center, with a population of about 80,000.[201] In 1898 the first Talmud Torah was opened. By 1917 there were five Talmud Torahs which were reorganized and combined with the United Talmud Torahs of Montreal.[202] In 1948–49 the Talmud Torahs had a total enrollment of 1,005 pupils. Their schools have classes which cover ten grades of the elementary school and junior and senior high school departments.[203] In 1949 there were three yeshivoth in Montreal, the Yeshivah Tmimim (Lubavitcher Yeshivah), the Yeshivah Merkaz Hatorah (Mirer Yeshivah), and the Meir Hagolah. All these yeshivoth follow a curriculum and are conducted in the traditional style of the eastern European yeshivoth. They aim at teaching the Jewish religion to their pupils, and this includes the teaching of the Shulchan Aruch.

CHAPTER VI

THE SHULCHAN ARUCH—ITS SIGNIFICANCE IN THE PAST—ITS EDUCATIONAL CONTENTS— ITS RECENT STATUS

The Shulchan Aruch, now the foremost religious code of Jewish law, has governed the life of religious Jews ever since its appearance in 1565. The Code has had a unifying effect upon traditional Jewry the world over, particularly after it was emended by Rabbi Moses Isserles to suit the needs not only of the Sephardic but also of the Ashkenazic Jews. Thus, the Shulchan Aruch gave unity also to the various interpretations of Biblical law disseminated at that period.

Written in direct language, the Code became a guide in the hands of the layman whose knowledge of the Hebrew language, and particularly of Hebrew law, had been reduced due to the persecutions and wanderings of the Jewish people at the time. Not only was the layman helped by the Shulchan Aruch, but the rabbi was also able to use the Code as a reference work, even if he did not wish to rely upon its decisions.

The Code was especially important in Jewish communities in Poland, Russia, and Lithuania, where it was given official status by the Council of the Four Lands in 1618.

From the point of view of education, the Code has been used as a text in yeshivoth, *i.e.*, in institutions of higher Jewish learning. In elementary schools, the laws of the Code were taught orally.

Before discussing the significance of the Shulchan Aruch in Jewish education today, it would be well to review the principles of education embodied in the Code as compared with those of modern education. The educational principles inherent in the Code relate to the harmonious development of the individual in relation to the development of his physical nature, of his mental capacities, and of his social behavior. The Code advocates these principles in its teaching of obedience to the Almighty and to the laws of the Torah.

The principles relating to the physical development of the individual include rest, health, and hygiene, food, and recreation. The Shulchan Aruch, unlike modern education where these principles occupy a prominent role, accords these physical principles a secondary place. However, aspects of physical care that are directly related to the teachings of the Torah, such as care of health, are of first importance in the Code.

In the Code, educational principles relating to the development of mental capacities of the individual are dealt with as arousal of interest, self-activity on the level of the learner, stimulating effort, motivation, individual differences, correlation of learning with inculcation of right attitudes and habits, and training of memory. Self-activity or learning by doing calls for participation in various social and religious activities and imitation of the sages. The Code applies these principles to the study of the Torah and to the acquisition of good habits and right attitudes. The Code, while recognizing individual differences, advocates that the slow learner be in the same class with others. In modern education, the gifted learner is to develop his capacities under special supervision, while the slow learner is relegated to a separate class. It might be pointed out here that this difference between the attitude of the Code and modern education stems perhaps from the fact that in the Code the individual is rewarded for his love for and devotion to the study of the Torah, rather than for achievement in scholarship. Everything depends upon one's intention.

The Code's attitude toward the slow learner might also be interpreted from the point of view of the influence the gifted might eventually exercise upon the slow learner, for the study in class is by group discussion in which the latter participates.

The educational principles of social development in the Code refer to such phases as respect for one's parents, teachers, and elders, and the community at large; respect for the Torah and its commandments, respect for historical events, and respect for non-Jewish members of the community. Responsibility toward the community and the government is included.

The Code makes no provision for the training of leaders. While the Code recognizes the importance of personal appearance and other aspects of the leader, it stresses good habits, good character, honesty, and fear of the Almighty. One's will and ability to lead are the main prerequisites for the leader. However, special training is required to acquaint the leader with the complexities of modern society.

In the Shulchan Aruch, secular studies are deemed necessary only to the extent to which these help in understanding the Bible and fulfilling its precepts. In modern public education, however, secular studies are of primary importance, as they help to understand better the physical and social environment. This difference in attitude between the Code and modern education toward secular studies seems to stem from the fact that the Code teaches that the world can be improved by turning one's thought and heart toward God and His Commandments. Secular education advocates social improvement by knowing and understanding the physical environment. Both, however, advocate the ideal, namely, effective living, which is to be achieved through education.

Both are aware of the importance of the proper size of class. The Code emphasizes that the number of students should not exceed twenty-five. In modern education, too, this number is regarded as normal except where special situations arise.

Concerning discipline, both the Code and modern education agree that the teacher should create favorable class conditions and proper student-teacher relations. Teaching materials are to be free from mistakes. Modern education stresses the importance of visual aids.

According to the Code, silent reading causes forgetfulness. The value of reading aloud is emphasized. In modern education, it is suggested that the oral reading should be emphasized in the early stages of learning.

Both the Code and modern education require the teacher to possess values and qualities such as would be worthy of emulation. The teacher's classroom attitude should be firm but friendly.

Regarding adult education, which is necessary for the benefit of the individual and society, both the Code and modern education stress this.

In the Code, the education of women is to be geared to managing the home and to the bringing up of children according to the religious precepts of the Torah. In modern education, the woman, in addition to preparing for home management, is free to follow the education career she chooses. This difference between the Code and modern education might be interpreted from the following point of view: In the Code, the woman is considered as the living spirit of the home. The father, away from home working much of the time, has less education responsibility for his children than the mother. Modern education accords women equal status with men in the acquisition of knowledge for a livelihood. On the whole, modern education seems to stress the importance of social well-being as above the well-being of the family.

Returning to the significance of the Code among Jews at the present time, the following results seem to have been outstanding in our study. The Code has had serious opposition from various segments of Jewry who felt that the Code is outmoded, and that at best only certain portions of it are acceptable to the requirements of modern society. On the other hand, Orthodox Jewry has followed the teachings of the Shulchan Aruch continuously since it first appeared, with little or no modification.

From about the last quarter of the nineteenth century, a time that marked the appearance of the Haskalah (enlightenment) movement to the present, the teachings of the Code have been either followed in part, modified considerably, or discarded entirely by various segments of the Jewish population. From about the middle of the twentieth century, with the gradual growth of Jewish education in the United States, there has been a marked movement to return to the teachings of the Shulchan Aruch. The following reasons for the return to the teachings of the Code might be ventured: The foundation of the state of Israel wrought many changes and one of these was the conclusion that secular education alone did not suffice for some Jews. Whatever the reasons for the movement toward the traditional teachings of the Code once again, it has been pointed out in our study that the Shulchan Aruch or some parts thereof are being included in the curricula of Jewish schools everywhere today.

A note of interest might be added in conclusion. This writer has learned recently that Justice Mosheh Silberg of the Supreme Court of Israel advocates the adoption of the Shulchan Aruch as the official guide in both civil and criminal law in Israel. Indeed, those sections of the Shulchan Aruch which deal with family life, marriage, and divorce, and personal relations, have served as the official codes of the State of Israel since its inception.

NOTES

Chapter I

1. The spelling of "Shulchan Aruch" varies with different authors. Thus, for instance, S.M. Dubnow, *History of the Jews in Russia and Poland*, Vol. I, p. 124 spells it "Shulchan Arukh"; H.L. Gordon, *The Life of Caro*, p. 29 *et paasim*, spells it "Shulhan Aruk"; C. Roun, *The Jews*, p. 225 *et paasim*, spells it "Shulhan Aruck"; and Ismar Elbogen, *A Century of Jewish life*, p. 191, spells it "Shulhan 'Aruk."
2. David de Sola Pool, "The Traditional Code of Jewish Education," *Menorah Journal*, June–July 1924, fol. 16, No. 3, p. 270.
3. A collection of Oral Laws collected and edited by Judah the Prince, ca. 200 C.E.
4. The Talmud contains the Mishnah and a commentary on the Mishnah.
5. Pool, *op. cit.*; *cf.* Maimonides, Introduction *Yad Hachazakah*, Vol. I, where a similar description of sources for his own work is found.
6. An alternative spelling of the name "Caro" is often "Karo." (See, for instance, Graetz, Goodblatt, Margolis, Waxman.)
7. The edict of expulsion from Spain had been signed March 31, 1492, and was to be effective as of July 1492. The Jewish date for the expulsion coincided with the Day of Fast of the Ninth of Ab. *Cf.* Nissan Waxman, Appendix to *Tomer Deborah*, by R. Moses Cordovero (1522–1570), p. 133.
8. Joseph Caro, Introduction to *Tur Orach Chayim* by Jacob ben Asher, *Cf.* Z'ev Yaavetz, *Toledoth Israel*, Vol. 13, p. 41.
9. Joseph Caro, *Shulchan Aruch-Orach Chayim*, Introduction.
10. Caro, *op. cit.* Caro compares the dissemination of conflicting decisions through the medium of printing to the case in the Talmud which states that "When the disciples of Shammai and Hillel who had not served [their teachers] sufficiently multiplied, dissensions increased in Israel, and the Torah became like two Toroth" [Sotah 47b]. Caro adds, however, that in the case of dissemination through printing the Torah became not like "two Toroth" but like numberless [conflicting] Toroth [Sotah 47b].
11. *Loc. cit.*
12. H. Graetz, *History of the Jews*, Vol. IV, p. 612. See also Jacob H. Marcus, *The Jew in the Medieval World. A Source Book, 315–1791*, p. 200.
13. Z'ev Yaavetz, *Toledoth Israel* (The History of the Jews), Vol. 13, p. 41.
14. Leopold Greenwald, *Harav R. Josef Caro Uzmano*, p. 177; also H. L. Gordon, *The Maggid of Caro*, p. 94. Aaron Sversky points out that Caro's decisions in the *Beth Yosef* represents the decisions of two hundred contemporary rabbis. *Cf.* Sversky, Introduction to *Maggid Maysharim* by Joseph Caro, p. 6. Also Hayyim David

Azulai, known as the ḤID'O, quotes Rabbi Hayyim Abulafia as saying that "anyone who follows the decisions of Rabbi Joseph Caro, follows in the footsteps of two hundred rabbis." See *Maarecheth Sefarim* appended to *Maarecheth Gedolim*, p. 8a.

15. Graetz, op. cit., pp. 612–613. See also Bezalel Landau, Introduction, *Sh'eloth U'Teshuvoth Beth Yosef*, who states that Caro's decisions have been "accepted in every Jewish house even for future generations."

16. It is of interest to note that Caro seems to have anticipated the Shulchan Aruch while writing the *Beth Yosef*, for he writes that the *Beth Yosef* will also be called Shulchan Aruch; see Joseph Caro, *Maggid Maysharim*, pp. 90 and 152. *Cf.* Harav Reuben Margolioth, *Defusay Hashulchan Aruch Harishonim; Sinai, Yarchon Lethorah, Lemada Ulesifruth*, Vol. XXXVII, Nisan Elul 1956, p. 25, note 2.

17. Joseph Caro, *Shulchan Aruch-Orach Chayim*, Introduction, states: "And I shall decide among the previous [opinions] . . . and if in a few countries certain things are decided differently, even though we shall decide to the contrary they will hold on to their customs for they already took upon themselves the decisions of their rabbi, and it is forbidden to them to change the existing custom." (free translation)

18. Meyer Waxman, *A History of Jewish Literature*, Vol. II, p. 147.

19. Louis Ginzberg, "Caro, Joseph B. Ephraim," *The Jewish Encyclopedia*, Vol. III, p. 586. It is interesting to note that Israel Zimberg (*Di Geszichte fun di Literatur bei Idn*, Vol. V, p. 51), ascribes the greater scrupulousness of the Ashkenazic Jews in religious matters to the fact that they "passed through generations of persecutions and expulsions."

20. Ginzberg, *op. cit.*, p. 586. Rabbi Reuven Margolioth in "Defusay HaShulchan Aruch HaRishonim" (The First Printings of the Shulchan Aruch), *Sinai*, Vol. XXXVII, pp. 25–35, gives the following dates *Shulchan Aruch-Orach Chayim* was printed in Venice 1565; *Shulchan Aruch-Yoreh Deah*, Venice, Nisan, 1565; *Shulchan Aruch-Eben Haezer*, Safed 1557 (Manuscript was finished); *Shulchan Aruch-Choshen Mishpat*, begun in Venice Heshvan 1565, finished on Friday (fifteen days), in Adar Rishon 1565.

21. Yaavetz, *op. cit.*, p. 39. *Cf.* also Moses Isserles, Introduction, *Shulchan Aruch-Orach Chayim*.

22. Zimberg, *op. cit.*, Vol. V, p. 50.

23. Joseph Caro, Introduction, *Shulchan Aruch-Choshen Mishpat*. Compare also *Shulchan Aruch-Orach Chayim*, 46:2, where Caro complains of the widespread ignorance. It may be noted here that some scholars feel that Caro's aspiration to authority, to revive ordination, and to hasten the coming of the Messiah, motivated him to write this code. See, for instance, Graetz, *op. cit.*, Vol. IV, pp. 538–539, and Greenwald, *op. cit.*, p. 137.

24. Caro, *loc. cit.*

25. Caro, *loc. cit.*

26. Waxman, *op. cit.*, Vol. II, p. 146.

27. Solomon Schechter, *Studies in Judaism*, p. 205. *Cf.* Simcha Asaf, *Mekorot Letoldoth Hachinuch BeIsrael*, (Sources of the History of Jewish Education), Introduction, p. 3.

28. Greenwald, *op. cit.*, p. 157. *Cf.* Israel Meir HaCohen (1838–1938), *Mishnah*

Brurah, Introduction, p. 6; and Graetz, *op. cit.*, Vol. IV, p. 613. Aaron Sversky states that the Shulchan Aruch "became the most famous and most reliable code after the Talmud . . . and every Jew ought to direct his steps according to the rules in the Code"; see Joseph Caro, Introduction, *Maggid Maysharim*, p. 8. We find a similar note to the effect that no other work in Judaism after the Talmud has been so widespread and accepted as the Shulchan Aruch, by Rav Tzair in *Haschiloah*, Vol. IV, Nos. 19–24, July–December 1898, p. 308.

29. Cecil Roth, *A Short History of the Jewish People*, p. 285.
30. Isserles, *op. cit.. Cf.* Yaavetz, Vol. XIII, pp. 44, 58, 87.
31. Israel Abrahams, *Jewish Life in the Middle Ages*, Introduction, p. xxv.
32. Leopold Greenwald, *Harav R. Yosef Caro Uzmano*, p. 175. *Cf.* Joseph S. Bloch, "The Shulchan Aruch-Its Origin, Validity, and Significance," *Israel and the Nations*, p. 59.
33. *Ibid.*, pp. 59–60. Moses Isserles, in his introduction to the *Shulchan Aruch-Choshen Mishpat*, Part II, states: "The author of the *Beth Yosef* and of the Shulchan Aruch left no room for improving upon the law except to point out differences in customs in these [Polish and German] countries." (free translation)
34. Waxman, *op. cit.*, Vol. II, p. 146.
35. H. Graetz, *History of the Jews*, Vol. V, p. 51, *Cf.* Yaavetz, *op. cit.*, p. 44.
36. Hirsch Loeb Gordon, *The Maggid of Caro*, p. 36, states: " . . . most of the facts of his (Caro's) life had to be presented for the first time, for lack of simple biographical data on Caro and his contemporaros."
37. Greenwald, *op. cit.*, p. 60.
38. Louis Ginzberg, "Caro, Joseph B. Ephraim," *Jewish Encyclopedia*, Vol. III, p. 583, and Waxman, *op. cit.*, p. 144, give the place of birth as "Spain or Portugal." Shlomo Ruzanis, *Divray Yemay Israel BeThogarma, 1300–1520* (The History of the Jews in Turkey, 1300–1520) gives the place of birth as Tulitula, Spain. (Second edition), Vol. I, p. 107.
39. Gordon, *op. cit.*, p. 50. Gordon also states: "The Caro family has also claimed descent from the royal house of King David."
40. *Ibid.*, p. 60, states: "The exact itinerary of Caro . . . is somewhat uncertain." Ginzberg, *op. cit.*, and Max L. Margolis, *A History of the Jewish People*, p. 520, maintain that Caro went from Spain to Turkey. Other writers avoid any definite statements.
41. Ruzanis, *op. cit.*, pp. 95–96 and 107, states that from Spain Caro's *father* (italics mine) went to Lisbon, thus implying that Caro's mother might have died before the family reached Portugal. In connection with this, Gordon, *op. cit.*, p. 290, states: "of Caro's mother we know nothing" which is significant.
42. Yaavetz, *op. cit.*, Vol. XIII, p. 41 (free translation).
43. Zimberg, *Di Geszichte fun di Literatur bei Idn*, Vol. IV, p. 275.
44. Meyer Waxman, *A History of Jewish Literature*, p. 144.
45. Jacob Pinchas Kohn, "Karo, Joseph," *The Universal Jewish Encyclopedia*, Vol. III, p. 49. Compare Ruzanis, *op. cit.*, p. 107.
46. Greenwald, *op. cit.*, p. 55.
47. S. Schechter, *Studies in Judaism*, Second Series, p. 210.

48. Aaron Sversky, Introduction to *Maggid Maysharim* by Joseph Caro, Jerusalem, 1960, p. 5.
49. Isidore Fishman, *The History of Jewish Education in Central Europe,* p. 77 states: "The child generally began his formal schooling at the age of five (and often) at three." Compare Gordon, *op. cit.,* p. 297, and Abraham A. Neumann, *The Jews in Spain,* Vol. II, p. 70.
50. Israel Elfenbein, "Jewish Education in Palestine under Turkey," *Brocho l'Mnachem,* p. 57, states: "It was the custom of the land to bring the lad to school at an early age of two or three years...."
51. See, for instance, *Deuteronomy* VI:7, "And thou shalt teach them diligently unto thy children, and shalt talk of them when thou sittest in thine house, and when thou walkest by the way, and when thou liest down, and when thou risest up." *The Pentateuch and Haftaroth,* Meir Halevi Leteris, Editor. Compare also *Deuteronomy* XI, 19.
52. Born at Avoda near Toledo, Spain in 1474, died at Safed, April 3, 1546.
53. Fishman, *op. cit.,* p. 86. Also Abraham A. Neuman, *The Jews in Spain,* Vol. II, p. 70, states: "At about the age of seven the bright Jewish boy was initiated in the study of the Mishnah... In the eighth year (he) was introduced to the study of the... Talmud."
54. Scholars disagree about the year of Caro's arrival in Turkey. Thus, for instance, Ruzanis, *op. cit.,* p. 109, maintains it was 1498; Gordon, *op. cit.,* p. 60, implies that it was 1496.
55. Scholars disagree about whether Caro's father settled first in Constantinople, as for instance, Ruzanis, *loc. cit.,* or Z'ev Yaavetz, *Toledoth Israel,* p. 41.
56. Ruzanis, *op. cit.,* pp. 107–108. *Halacha* refers to the legal parts of the Talmudic and Rabbinic literatures.
57. H. L. Gordon, *The Maggid of Caro,* p. 62
58. Joseph Caro, Introduction to *Yad Hachazakah,* (The Strong Hand), by Moses ben Maimon. The words "Keseph Mishneh" Caro explains to mean a "double lounging."
59. Greenwald, *op. cit.,* p. 54, says that it is not known whether Isaac Caro (Caro's uncle) went to Palestine.
60. Gordon, *op. cit.,* p. 64. Note that while Ruzanis, *op. cit.,* p. 141, maintains that Caro went to establish, not to head, a rabbinical academy, Zimberg, *op. cit.,* Vol. IV, p. 275, states that Caro went there to officiate as a rabbi.
61. Yaavetz, *op. cit.,* pp. 40–42.
62. Gordon, *op. cit.,* p. 70. Also Greenwald, *op. cit.,* p. 160. Shlomo Ruzanis notes that in Adrianople, Caro was the most outstanding Jewish authority of that generation. *Cf. Divray Yemay Israel BeThogarma 1300–1520,* (The History of the Jews in Turkey 1300–1520).
63. S. Schechter, *Studies in Judaism,* Second Series, p. 118. *Cf.* Gordon, *op. cit.,* p. 81. 1535 and 1536 are dates given by other writers. It may be of interest to note here that according to Yehudah Avida, *Rishoney Mishpachat Caro B'Eretz Israel* (The First Settlers of the Caro Family in Israel), p. 131: "Joseph Caro was... the fourth member of his family to settle in Israel." Nissim Waxman remarks that one of the major reasons why Safed became a center of spiritual Judaism was the fact that

there were no monasteries or other non-Jewish places of worship. *Cf.* Appendix, *Tomer Deborah*, by R. Moses Cordovero (1522–1570), p. 136.
64. Yaavetz, *op. cit.*, p. 42, states that Joseph Caro tended toward the mystical. *Cf.* Gordon, *op. cit.*, p. 61. Note that Mary W. Montgomery, "Turkey," *The Jewish Encyclopedia*, XII, p. 282, writes that the Jews of Turkey considered their prosperity as a sign of the coming of the Messiah
65. Gordon, *op. cit.*, p. 81.
66. *Loc. Cit.* Gordon writes: "As the Messiah was expected in 1540 and Safed was expected to be the center of the messianic millennial drama, Caro hurried thither, arriving in 1536."
67. Zev Yaavetz, *Toledoth Israel*, p. 40. W. L. Margolis and A. Marx, *A History of the Jewish People*, p. 519. Compare Louis Ginzberg, "Caro, Joseph B. Ephraim," *The Jewish Encyclopedia*, Vol. III, p. 583. Note that ordination transmitted to the ordained the right to act as a rabbi and judge in matters religious and legal. It was abolished by Rome after Bar Kochba's rebellion, ca. 135 C.E. See also Simon M. Dubnow, *History of the Jews in Russia and Poland*, Vol. III, p. 182.
68. H. Graetz, *History of the Jews*, Vol. IV, p. 538.
69. Yaavetz, *op. cit.*, p. 46. *Cf.* Gordon, *op. cit.*, p. 93.
70. Yaavetz, *op. cit.*, p. 42. *Cf.* Jacob Pinchas Kohn, "Caro, Joseph," *The Universal Jewish Encyclopedia*, p. 49. H. L. Gordon, *The Maggid of Caro*, p. 70, gives the Jewish date as 11 Elul, 5302. *Cf.* David Ashkenazi, *Korei Hadoroth*, pp. 63–64, who comments that Joseph Caro was the greatest figure of his generation. He settled in Nicopolis and later moved to Adrianople where he began his *Beth Yoseph* in 1522 and completed it in Safed in 1542. He then edited and made corrections, a task that took him another twelve years. On his way to Safed he passed through Salonika. In Safed he studied in the Beth Hamidrash of R. Yaacov ben Rav.
71. Besides the writings mentioned, Caro composed a number of other works. The list which follows is taken from Gordon, *op. cit.*, pp. 98–99. *Cf.* Simcha Asaf, *Mekoroth Letoledoth Hachinuch Belsrael*, Preface, p. iii.

Books Printed in His Lifetime

Beth Yoseph, commentary on the Turim. Composition began in Adrianople, 1522; completed in Safed, 1542; final revision, 1554 (Venice, 1550–1551, Sabionetta 1553–1559).

Kesef Mishnah, commentary on Maimonides' *Yad Hachazakah;* composed in Nicopolis (Venice, 1574–1575).

Shulchan Aruch, composed in Safed; completed in 1556 (Venice, 1565).

Books Printed after His Death

Avkat Rochel, responsa (Smyrna, 1790).

Bedek Habbayit, corrections and supplements to *Beth Yoseph*, (Salonika, 1605).

Derashot (also called *Or Zaddikkim*), homilies (Salonika, 1792).

Kelaley ha-Talmud (also called Kelaley ha-Gemara), hermanentics of the Talmud (Salonika, 1598).

Maggid Maysharim, diary (first edition, Lublin, 1646).

Teshuvoth, responsa (Salonika, 1599).

Writings Lost

Commentary on the Mishnah, composed in Nicopolis.
Supercommentary on Rashi (1040–1105).
Supercommentary on Asheri (1230–1328).
Supercommentary on Maimonides (1195–1270).

Letter, signed by Caro, found in Cambridge University Library, undated; it is marked F.S. 13/2428, and is reported by Simcha Asaf in *Sinai,* Yarchon LaTorah, LeMada UleSifruth, 3rd year, Vol. VI, copies 7-38, dated Kislev-Yian, 1940, pp. 117–118; Jerusalem; Mosad Harav Kuk, I. L. HaCohen Fishman, Editor. In this letter Caro asks an Egyptian Jew to defray some money to the widow of Rabbi Shelomo Sirilin, d. ca. 1554.

72. Gordon, *op. cit.,* p. 50.
73. No date is available for the death of Caro's second wife.
74. Gordon, *op. cit.,* p. 261, gives the date of birth of Caro's son, Judah, as 15 Elas, 5329 (August 4, 1569). Gordon also states (*op. cit.,* p. 99) that Caro had a daughter, Tammah, "... whose progeny is unknown, [and that] two other sons and one daughter died during his lifetime." Aaron Sversky states that in Salonika, during an epidemic, all three of Caro's children died. (*Cf.* Introduction to *Maggid Maysharim* by Joseph Caro, p. 6.) Caro mentions that his son Yehudah was circumcised on the 15th of Elul of the year 1569, a week after birth. (Joseph Caro, *Sefer Maggid Maysharim,* pp. 137–138.)
75. Gordon, *op. cit.,* 101. The date of Caro's death is variously given as Thursday, Nisan 13, (May 1575) (S. Ruzanis, *Divrey Yemay Israel BeThogarma,* p. 107, note 76); Nisan 13, 1575, (L. Greenwald, *Harav R'Yosef Caro Uzmano,* p. 129; Nisan (April) 1575, (R. Graetz, *History of the Jews,* Vol. IV, p. 616); and March 24, 1575, (L. Ginzberg, "Caro, Joseph B. Ephraim," *The Jewish Encyclopedia,* Vol. III, p. 583. Zimberg describes Joseph Caro as "a classical example of one who directed all his efforts toward collecting and preserving with deep love the entire Jewish religious inheritance of past generations ..." (free translation). *Cf.* Zimberg, *Di Geszichte fun der Literatur bei idn,* Vol. V, pp. 48–49.
76. Reference is to Judah the Prince, the compiler of the *Mishnah,* ca. 134–ca. 220 C.E.
77. Sukkah, 28a, *Seder Moed,* Vol. VI, p. 122.
78. See, for instance, Morris H. Goodblatt, *Jewish Life in Turkey in the XVIth Century,* Preface, p. xi.
79. *Ibid.,* p. 3.
80. Mary W. Montgomery, "Turkey," *Jewish Encyclopedia,* Vol. III, p. 281. See also Jacob R. Marcus, *The Jew in the Medieval World: A Source Book,* 315–1791, p. 53, and particularly p. 413 where he quotes from the German diary of Hans Dernschwan, Bohemia, 1494. Compare also, Ernest Maintz, *Les Juifs d'Alger sous la Domination Turque* (The Jews of Algeria under Turkish rule), p. 13 ff.
81. Cecil Roth, "The European Age in Jewish History," *The Jews,* Vol. I, p. 245.
82. A discussion of Jewish education in Palestine follows later in the chapter.
83. Israel Abrahams, *Jewish Life in the Middle Ages,* pp. 341 and 357.
84. Julius B. Maller, "The Role of Education in Jewish History," *The Jews,* Vol. II, p. 906. Compare also Abrahams, *ibid.,* p. 341.

85. Gordon, *op. cit.*, p. 297; see also Isidore Fishman, *The History of Jewish Education in Central Europe*, p. 92.
86. See, for instance, *Shulchan Aruch-Yoreh Deah*, 245:8, where Rabbi Moses Isserles quoting Isaac Abrabanel (Lisbon 1437–Venice, 1528) remarks that a child should be taught the Hebrew alphabet before the age of three, so that he accustoms himself to read the Torah.
87. Abrahams, *op. cit.*, p. 351. See also Nathan Drazin, *History of Jewish Education from 515 B.C.E. to 330 C.E.*, p. 82, and Fishman, *op. cit.*, p. 94, referring to *Leviticus Rabbah* VII, 3, Louis Ginzberg, *Students, Scholars, and Saints*, p. 23.
88. The Pentateuch is divided into weekly cycles calculated to be read within a year in the synagogue and studied in the elementary schools. Compare Abraham A. Neuman, *The Jews in Spain*, Vol. II, p. 70.
89. Abrahams, *op. cit.*, pp. 248–349. Compare also Drazin, *op. cit.*, p. 81. Also, in his Preface, p. vii, Drazin notes that by C.E. 220, "The Jewish school was fully evolved and tested."
90. Joseph R. Marcus, *The Jew in the Medieval World; A Source Book*, 315–1791, pp. 374 and 378; Israel Zimberg, *Di Geszichte fun der Literatur bei idn*, Vol. IV, p. 263; Abrahams, *op. cit.*, p. 369; and Mailer, *op. cit.*, p. 906.
91. Abrahams, *op. cit.*, pp. 359 and 369 ff.
92. Simcha Asaf, *Mekoroth Letoledoth Hachinuch BeIsrael*, Vol. III, pp. 11–14.
93. Published in Salonica, 1564.
94. Asaf, *op. cit.*, p. 60.
95. First published at Wandebak, 1733.
96. H. Graetz, *History of the Jews*, Vol. III, p. 572.
97. Maller, *op. cit.*, Vol. II, p. 906. See also Graetz, *ibid.*, p. 446: "The northern French Jews were too exclusively absorbed in the Talmud." See also *ibid.*, p. 290.
98. Rabbi Isaac of Karlin, 1662–1726, states: "I thank the Almighty who freed me from the responsibility of the times, almost from my childhood. And my wife supported me and the house from her own work. May the Almighty Bless her and her children that she may see their happiness and the happiness of His people." *Cf.* Introduction to *Keren Orah, Chidushei Halachoth al Masecheth Yevamoth*.
99. Drazin, *op. cit.*, p. 14. *Cf.* Lewis Joseph Sherrill, *The Rise of Christian Education*, p. 63.
100. *Ibid.* (Drazin), pp. 129 ff.
101. Israel Abrahams, *Jewish life in the Middle Ages*, p. 342. Compare also Drazin, *op. cit.*, pp. 129 ff.
102. Asaf, *op. cit.*, p. 74.
103. Published in Salonica, 1769.
104. Abdul H. N. Sassani, *Education in turkey*, pp. 2–3. See also Ernest Maintz, *Les Juifs d'Alger sous la Domination Turque*, pp. 197, 198, and 204.
105. Sassani, *op. cit.*, p. 9.
106. Frank Pierrepont Graves, *A History of Education*, pp. 40–46.
107. Graves, *op. cit.* See also Sassani, *op. cit.*, p. 8.
108. Bernette Miller, *The Palace School of Mohammad, the Conqueror*, pp. 4–7 and 19.
109. *Ibid.*, p. 94, as quoted in Menavini's *Trattato*, p. 91.

110. Miller, *op. cit.*, p. 36.
111. Sassani, *op. cit.*, p. 5. See also, Herbert Adams Gibbons, *The Foundation of the Ottoman Empire*, p. 75.
112. Sassani, *loc. cit.*
113. Morris S. Goodblatt, *Jewish Life in Turkey in the XVIth Century*, p. 108, writes that with regard to law and ritual, "the rabbis of Salonica and Constantinople were not ready to submit to their colleagues in Safed or Jerusalem."
114. Schechter, *op. cit.*, p. 203.
115. Solomon Schechter, *Studies in Judaism*, Second Series, 1908, *Cf.* Simcha Asaf, *Mekoroth Letoledoth Hachinuch BeIsrael*, Vol. III, Introduction, p. iii.
116. Full name is Rabbi Isaac ben Solomon Ashkenazi Loria (also spelled Luria, as in passage just quoted), better known in Talmudic circles as "the Ari" (the Lion).
117. Schechter, *op. cit.*, p. 209.
118. Ref. to Shlomel (also spelled "Shlumel"), 43a. *Cf.* Asaf, *op. cit.*, p. 27 and p. 25 concerning R. Zecharia b-Saadiah's description of Safed during the time of Joseph Caro.
119. Schechter, *op. cit.*, p. 230.
120. Asaf, *op. cit.*, Vol. III, p. 14.
121. Asaf, *op. cit.*, Asaf quotes Rabbi Solomon Ephrayim Luntschitz from his work *Oleloth Ephraim*, written in 1607, to the effect that "the student body of Eretz Israel (Palestine) and of those countries that follow the way of teaching in Palestine, is much superior to that of Germany and Poland."
122. In *B'rocho L'Mnachem*, Festive Edition, 1955, pp. 63–70.
123. *Ibid.*, p. 54, referring to Zahalon, Responsa No. 75. *Cf. Shulchan Aruch-Yoreh Deah*, 245:17.
124. *Cf. Shulchan Aruch-Yoreh Deah*, 243:1–3.
125. Elfenbein, *op. cit.*, p. 57. *Cf. Shulchan Aruch-Yoreh Deah*, 245:5.
126. Elfenbein, *op. cit.*, p. 57. Reference is to Eliahu ben R. Mosheh Vidas' work *Reshith Hokma*, 1.c/1 Cf. Asaf, *op. cit.*, Vol. III, p. 19 where he quotes Rabbi Mosheh ben Makir of Safed from his work *Seder Hayom*, printed in Venice, 1599, (during the lifetime of the author) to the effect that children should be taught the alphabet at the age of two or three. *Cf.* Asaf, *op. cit.*, p. 87.
127. Elfenbein, *op. cit.*, p. 59. Reference is to Mosheh ben Makir, *Seder Hayom*. *Cf.* Shulchan Aruch, *op. cit.*, 245;5 where it is suggested that the child be brought to school between the ages of six and seven.
128. Elfenbein, *op. cit.*, p. 57. Ref. Hagiz. *Cf.* Asaf, *op. cit.*, pp. 5, 15, 19–20, 25–26, 29, 32, 54–55 and 87.
129. Also spelled *Haggadah*, meaning stories, tales, referring to the non-legal part of the old rabbinic literature.
130. Elfenbein, *op. cit.*, p. 58. Ref. is to Hagiz, 2.c/9a. *Cf.* Asaf, *op. cit.*, pp. 5, 10, 15, 19–20, 25–26, 29, 32, 54–55, 87.
131. Elfenbein, *op. cit.*, p. 58. Reference is to *Seder Hayom*, 48, note 2.
132. *Loc. cit.*
133. Elfenbein, *op. cit.*, pp. 58–59. Reference is to Moses Hagiz in the name of his father, in *Mishnat Hakamim*, 9 a-a.

134. Reference is to his preface in commentary on the Pentateuch. See Elfenbein, *op. cit.*, p. 59.
135. Reference is to the Yeshivah founded by Rabbi itzchak ben Shulel Ha-Cohen. See Asaf, *op. cit.*, pp. 9–10; Elfenbein, *op. cit.*, p. 60, referring to Neubauer, Lebanon, XXVI: Hama'amar III, 199.
136. Israel Elfenbein, "Jewish Education in Palestine under Turkey," *Brocho L'Mnachem*, p. 60. Note, however, that Asaf, *op. cit.* Vol. III, p. 10, states that they covered daily "two folios or one and a half folios."
137. *Cf.* Asaf, *op. cit.*, p. 29 *et passim*.
138. See, for instance, Asaf, *op. cit.*, pp. 19–20 and 87. Reference is to *Seder Nezikin*, Vol. VIII, pp. 74–75.
139. Elfenbein, *op. cit.*, p. 53. See also Asaf, *op. cit.*, p. 26.
140. Elfenbein, *loc. cit.*
141. Solomon Schechter, *Studies in Judaism*, Second Series, 1908, p. 243.
142. Elfenbein points out, however, that Schechter, among others, leaves the impression that "the only profession for which there was no room in Palestine was that of a private tutor." *Op. cit.*, p. 53.
143. Asaf, *op. cit.*, p. 25.
144. *Ibid.*, p. 27.
145. Asaf, *op. cit.*, Vol. III, pp. 27 and 31.
146. Israel Elfenbein, *Brocho L'Mnachem*, p. 56. Reference is to Hakam Zechariah Sephardi in 1495 (Jerusalem III, 2, Ham. III, 165).
147. Gershom G. Sholem, *Major Trends in Jewish Mysticism*, p. 320.
148. Israel Abrahams, *Jewish life in the Middle Ages*, p. 351; *Cf.* also Nathan Drazin, *History of Jewish Education from 515 B.C.E. to 220 C.E.*, p. 82; Isidore Fishman, *The History of Jewish Education in Central Europe*, p. 94; and Louis Ginzberg, *Students, Scholars and Saints*, p. 23.
149. Quoted in Schechter, *op. cit.*, pp. 292–294.
150. *Ibid.*, p. 294.
151. *Ibid.*, p. 296.

Chapter II

1. C.E. Turner, *Principles of Health Education*, p. 70, points out: "The child should think of health as a matter of conduct not as a subject of instruction." See also *ibid.*, p. 193, for a similar principle. *Cf.* Herbert G. Lull, *Principles of Elementary Education*, p. 475, who points out that health attitudes and health habits are important for the teachers, the parents, and the children. Philip W.L. Cox and Forrest E. Long, *Principles of Secondary Education*, p. 381, observe that "habit formation is the basis of all learning."
2. *Shulchan Aruch-Yoreh Deah*, 336:1. See also *Shulchan Aruch-Orach Chayim*, 39:4, where the hungry and the thirsty are included among the sick. Biblical reference is to *Exodus* XXI, 19.
3. *Shulchan Aruch-Orach Chayim*, 329:1. See also *ibid.*, 238:12 ff. See also *Leviticus* XVIII, 5. Lull, *op. cit.*, page 163, points out that in the elementary grades health instruction should concern itself chiefly with social sanitation and health, food selection, regularity in eating, and infections from foods and drinks.
4. *Shulchan Aruch-Orach Chayim*, 278:1.
5. *Ibid.*, 318:2.
6. A fast day commemorating the destruction of the Temple.
7. *Shulchan Aruch-Orach Chayim*, 354:11, 554:9 and 14.
8. *Ibid.*, 614:1. See also *ibid.*, 554:6, 640:3–4, and 692:4 for similar rules.
9. *Ibid.*, 618:9. See also *ibid.*, 204:9, 613:4, and 617:3. Note that observation of symptoms and the rule of flexibility are here involved.
10. *Ibid.*, 616:1–2. Note that an attitude toward preventive health measures is here involved.
11. *Shulchan Aruch-Orach Chayim*, 276:5.
12. Turner, *op. cit.*, p. 168, points out: "Cleanliness and neatness ... represent a quality of behavior that engenders social ease and self-respect."
13. *Ibid.*, p. 167. Turner notes: "Hand-washing and the avoidance of nail-biting are valuable practices in preventive hygiene."
14. *Ibid.*, 4:18; see also *ibid.*, 4:1, 3, 4, and 319:10 and 16.
15. *Ibid.*, 4:3. See also *ibid.*, 4:17 and 21.
16. *Ibid.*, 170:16. For other preventive health measures see *ibid.*, 3:9, 4:20, 170:1, 15, 22, 175:5, 471:1 and 529:2. Compare also *Shulchan Aruch-Yorah Deah*, 116Z:2. See also *Maseket Derek Erez* (Treatise on Ethics), p. 75: "One should not offer his neighbor a drink from the cup from which he has first drunk, for it may prove dangerous." Note also Turner, *op. cit.*, p. 53: "Preventive medicine and preventive sanitation are of fundamental value ... we must rely upon preventive hygiene."

17. *Shulchan Aruch-Orach Chayim*, 160:1, 9, 319:16. Compare also *Maseket Derek Erez, op. cit.*, p. 115: "He who... drinks water that has been kept uncovered overnight, risks his life, because of the danger involved."
18. *Ibid.*, 167:1–9, *Cf. Aboth* III, 3. "R. SIMEON SAID: IF THREE HAVE EATEN AT ONE TABLE AND HAVE NOT SPOKEN THE GREAT WORDS OF TORAH, [IT IS] AS IF THEY HAD EATEN SACRIFICES [OFFERED] TO THE DEAD." The Babylonian Talmud, Seder Nezikin, Vol. VIII, p. 28.
19. *Ibid.*, 202:4, where it is pointed out that drinking olive oil is harmful. See also *ibid.*, 202:5–6, 12, 16, 204:1, and 208:3, *Deuteronomy* XXIII, 11–15 and *Yoma* 18a.
20. *Ibid.*, 157:1.
21. Additional morning services.
22. *Shulchan Aruch-Orach Chayim*, 286:3 and 288:3.
23. *Ibid.*, 608:4.
24. *Shulchan Aruch-Orach Chayim*, 179:6, and 301:23.
25. Philip R.V. Curoe, *Principles of Education*, p. 25.
26. *Shulchan Aruch-Orach Chayim*, 301:2.
27. *Ibid.*, 308:45. *Cf.* H.H. Horne, *The Psychological Principles of Education*, p. 379: "The Child must [learn] abstinence from certain games on Sunday."
28. *Loc. Cit.* See the commentary *Mishnah Berurah* on this law.
29. *Shulchan Aruch-Orach Chayim*, 328:42 and 338:1.
30. *Ibid.*, 301:2.
31. *Ibid.*, 339:2. See also *ibid.*, 252:1, 305:5, 308:19, and 316:3, 7, and 10.
32. *Ibid.*, 339:3.
33. *Ibid.*, 538:3. See also *ibid.*, 301:7, 316:1, 339:6, 495:2, 544:1 and 2.
34. Intermediate days are semi-holy days during which time certain work is permitted.
35. *Shulchan Aruch-Orach Chayim*, 536:1.
36. *Ibid.*, 340:4. This particular rule may even be interpreted as evidence of informal educational activity. Compare Morris Raphael Cohen, *A Dreamer's Journey* (Autobiography), pp. 31–32, where he states: "A good deal of my practice writing was done with my finger... on the surface of a box of sand to save the cost of paper...."
37. *Ibid.*, 301:20.
38. J. Donald Butler in his work *Four Philosophies and their Practice in Education and Religion*, New York: Harper and Brothers, 1957, p. 253, notes that character education lies at the core of what he calls "idealist education."
39. Herman Harrell Horne, *The Psychological Principles of Education*, p. 324.
40. *Shulchan Aruch-Yoreh Deah*, 251:9 where in distributing charity the learned man of illegitimate issue is preferred to "the ignorant high priest."
41. An important "means of arousing an attitude of interest toward school work is the emphasis on the value of what is taught... Interest gives a feeling of a sense of worth...." Paul Klapper, *Principles of Educational Practice*, p. 224. Compare also Aboth, *Seder Nezikin*, Vol. VIII, p. 629: "Which is the right course a man should choose for himself? That which is an honor to him who does it, and which also brings honor from mankind." See also *Proverbs*, IV, 13: "Take fast hold of correction; let *her* not go: Keep her; for she *is* thy life."

42. *Ibid.*, p. 232.
43. *Ibid.*
44. *Shulchan Aruch-Yoreh Dea*, 246:23. Compare *Deuteronomy* XI, 19, "And ye shall teach them your children . . . when thou liest down, and when thou risest up."
45. *Shulchan Aruch-Orach Chayim*, 238:1.
46. *Shulchan Aruch-Yoreh Deah*, 246:24.
47. *Ibid.*, 246:21. Compare aboth, *op. cit.*, VI, 4, pp. 82–83: "Such is the way of life conducive to the study of the Torah: a morsel of bread with salt thou shalt eat, and water by measure thou shalt drink, and upon the ground thou shalt sleep. . . ."
48. Note that all references in this thesis to the Babylonian Talmud are to the English translation of the Soncino Press.
49. *Shulchan Aruch-Yoreh Deah*, 246:25. Compare Aboth III, 7, *op. cit.*, p. 36: " . . . R. Simeon said: when one, walking on the road, rehearses [what he has learned] and breaks off from his rehearsing and says, 'How fine is this tree!' [or] 'How fine is this newly ploughed field!' Scripture accounts it to him as if he had incurred guilt [expiable] by his life."
50. *Shulchan Aruch-Yoreh Deah*, 246:18. Compare Aboth I, 17, *op. cit.*, p. 9: "Simeon the son [of Rabban Gamaliel] used to say: All my days I grew up among the sages, and I have found nothing better for a person than silence. Study is not the most important thing, but deed." See also L. Ginzberg, *Students, Scholars and Saints*, p. 27: "Religion to be a vital influence must be lived, not taught."
51. *Shulchan Aruch-Orach Chayim*, 90:14. See also section on respect for parents.
52. *Ibid.*, 90:12. See also *ibid.*, 301:1.
53. *Loc. cit.*
54. *Shulchan Aruch-Yoreh Deah*, 249:8. Note C.E. Turner, *Principles of Health Education*, p. 74: "The tendency of children to imitate those whom they admire is so strong that it may be used as a force in developing . . . behavior."
55. *Shulchan Aruch-Orach Chayim*, 28:3.
56. *Ibid.*, 4:16.
57. *Ibid.*, 65:3.
58. *Ibid.*, 89:1.
59. Horne, *op. cit.*, p. 379. Compare Louis Ginzberg, *op. cit.*, p. 23, "It was a cherished purpose to have the child say the prayers by himself . . . no attention was paid to their meaning, until he could read them fluently, on the principle that a hcild was first to be religiously active, and religious thinking would follow as his intelligence developed with years."
60. With the pronunciation of the name of God.
61. *Shulchan Aruch-Orach Chayim*, 215:3. See also *ibid.*, 128:34, 145:2, and 186:2.
62. Paul A. McGhee, "Higher Education and Adult Education: Four Questions," *Current Issues in Higher Education*, 1953, p. 202, points out that " . . . to be fully creative or productive, one must feel *involved . . . and participate.*" Cox and Long, *Principles of Secondary Education*, p. 218, notes that a curriculum must be calculated to "affect the school community institutions and activities."
63. *Shulchan Aruch-Orach Chayim*, 73:3. See also *ibid.*, 199:10, 366:3, and 589:1. Compare also Isaiah 38:19, "The father to the children shall make known the truth." See also Isidore Fishman, *Jewish Education in Central Europe*, p. 75: "At

an early age the boy was allowed to wind the phylacteries." Similarly Ginzberg, *op. cit.*, p. 16: "... the little fellow was given at an early age the Arba-Kanfot (Fringes, *Numbers* XV, 38) as part of his first boy's suit."

64. A palm branch, one of the four species of plants, the other three being myrtle-twigs, willow branches and a citron (see Leviticus XXIII:40) used on the feast of Tabernacles. See also Ginzberg, *op. cit.*, p. 16: "Shaking the lulav on Sukkoth (Feast of Tabernacles)... and many other customs prepared the child admirably for the more serious instruction in the Heder (elementary school)."
65. *Shulchan Aruch-orach Chayim*, 657:1, 675:3, and 677:2. Chanukah means the Feast of Lights.
66. *Ibid.*, 201:1.
67. Paul Klapper, *Principles of Educational Practice*, p. 195. Compare C.E. Turner, *Principles of Health Education*, p. 74: "The tendency of children to imitate those whom they admire is so strong that it may be used as a force in developing behavior." (See note 1 above.)
68. *Shulchan Aruch-Orach Chayim*, 199:6.
69. *Ibid.*, 53:10. Note that communal activity is here involved.
70. *Shulchan Aruch-Orach Chayim*, 460:1. Reference is to RaSH, initials of Rabbi Asher (ben Yechiel), b. Germany, ca. 1250, d. Toledo, Spain, 1328.
71. *Ibid.*, 460:2.
72. *Ibid.*, 250:1. Reference is to the expounders of the Mishnah (Talmud) who lived between 270–352. See M. Mielziner, *Introduction to the Talmud*, pp. 49–50.
73. *Shulchan Aruch-Orach Chayim*, 107:4.
74. Philip H.W. Curoe, *Principles of Education*, p. 59.
75. *Ibid.*, p. 60. J. Donald Butler, *Four Philosophies and their Practice in Education and Religion*, p. 372, points out: "The essence of teaching method is in matching *possible learning* tasks with the levels of abstraction of which the pupil is capable." Herbert G. Lull, *Principles of Elementary Education*, p. 85, notes that a curriculum designed "to pass on the elements of the social heritage to children" should take under consideration "individual differences and capacities."
76. *Shulchan Aruch-Yoreh Deah*, 245:2. (Free translation.) Compare also Ruth Strang, *An Introduction to Child Study*, Fourth Edition, New York: The Macmillan Company, 1939, p. 342: "The gifted child should have the opportunity to learn as fast and as much as he wants to, at any stage of his development." See also Mildred G. Fox, "Providing for the Gifted," *The Education Digest*, Vol. XIX, no. 6, February 1954, p. 10, quoting G.W. Whipple: "If any nation is destined to perish, it is the one that fails to provide the best educational opportunities for those who show promise of leadership."
77. *Shulchan Aruch-Yoreh Deah*, 245:9. Compare also L. Ginzberg, *Students, Scholars and Saints*, p. 33, to the effect that in the elementary school "... the instructor devoted himself to teaching as much of each week's Pentateuchal portion as the pupil's capacity permitted." Compare also *Proverbs* XXII:6.
78. *Ibid.*, 246:11. Compare *Maseket Derek Erez*, pp. 36–37: "If you desire to understand the Torah, do not say regarding that which you do not understand, I do understand; when you are taught and you do not understand, be not ashamed to say, I do not understand."

79. Literally, "House of Study."
80. *Shulchan Aruch-Yoreh Deah*, 246:11. Compare Aboth, II, 5, *Nezikin*, Vol. VIII, p. 15. *Cf.* Aboth V, 12, p. 68: "[There are] four types of character among disciples... slow to comprehend and quick to forget... slow to comprehend and slow to forget... quick to comprehend and slow to forget... slow to comprehend and quick to forget." "[There are] four types of character among those that sit before sages: [they are severally typified by] a sponge, a funnel, a strainer and a sieve: a sponge which absorbs all; a funnel which lets in at one end and lets out at the other; a strainer which lets out the wine and retains the lees; a sieve, which lets out the coarse meal and retains the choice flour." *Ibid.*, V, 15, p. 69.
81. *Ibid.*, 246:10.
82. Repetitio est mater studiorum—H.H. Horne, *The Psychological Principles of Education*, p. 117, quoting the Jesuit motto.
83. *Shulchan Aruch-Orach Chayim*, 285:1.
84. *Shulchan Aruch-Yoreh Deah*, 246:3.
85. *Loc. cit.* Reference is to *Deuteronomy* IV:9.
86. Specially prepared bread for the Sabbath, of which the Priest received a share.
87. *Shulchan Aruch-Yoreh Deah*, 522:3.
88. Horne, *op. cit.*, p. 121. Note that the association here is formed by the words *judge, choked,* and *life* as indicated on the following page.
89. "The case of an animal in whose body an organ is found to be absent or destroyed," (Marcus Jastrow, *A Dictionary of the Targumin, the Talmud Babli and Yerushalmi and the Midrashic Literature,* Vol. II, p. 848.
90. *Shulchan Aruch-Yoreh Deah*, 294.
91. Paul Klapper, *Principles of Educational Practice*, p. 248. See also Horne, *op. cit.*, p. 353: "The religious training... will consist of permitting only good things, forbidding only evil things."
92. *Shulchan Aruch-Orach Chayim*, 1:1 (free translation). Compare *ibid.*, 55:5, 106:2, 284:4, 343:3, 650:2, and 689:1 and 10. For other illustrations of this attitude, see the examples cited in the section in this chapter on stimulation of effort.
93. *Ibid.*, 238:2.
94. *Shulchan Aruch-Orach Chayim*, 98:1, also *ibid.*, 98:2–5. L.S. Sherrill, *The Rise of Christian Education*, p. 19, states: "... customs have become 'morals,' surrounded with the conviction that the will of God penetrates into every nook and cranny of existence."
95. *Shulchan Aruch-Orach Chayim, loc. cit.*
96. *Shulchan Aruch-Yoreh Deah*, 276:3.
97. *Ibid.*, 282:2.
98. "... habits can be inculcated by a process of repetition." Paul Klapper, *Principles of Educational Practice*, p. 448.
99. *Shulchan Aruch-Orach Chayim*, 610–4.
101. *Ibid.*, 262:1. See also *ibid.*, 231:1, and 263:1. Note that foresight is here involved.
102. *Shulchan Aruch-Orach Chayim:* 529:2 (free translation).
103. *Ibid.*, 322:6. Compare Aboth, I, 18, *Nezikim*, Vol. VIII, p. 10. "Rabban Simeon, son of Gamaliel used to say: on three things does the world stand: on justice on

truth, and on peace, as it is said: Judge ye truthfully and a judgment of peace in your gates." (*Zechariah* VIII, 16) Compare Sanhedrin 1, 27a, p. 162, *Seder Nezikim,* Vol. V: "Those are ineligible to be witnesses of judge: a gambler with dice, usurers . . ." See also C.E. Turner, *Principles of Health Education,* p. 81: "We want the child to recognize that to be truthful is more important than to report a perfect health record."

104. *Shulchan Aruch-Yoreh Deah* 247:2, (free translation) Compare *ibid.,* 217:1, 3, 4, 248:8, 249:2, 259:3, and *Shulchan Aruch-Choshen Mishpat* 97:1.

105. *Shulchan Aruch-Yoreh Deah,* 255:1. Compare Aboth I, 10, *op. cit.,* p. 7: "Shemaiah used to say: Love work, hate acting the superior . . ." See also *ibid,* II, 2, p. 12: "Rabban Gamaliel the son of R. Judah the Patriarch said: Excellent is the study of the Torah together with a worldly occupation, for the energy [taken up] by both of them keeps sin out of one's mind, and [as for] all [study of the] Torah where there is no worldly occupation, the end thereof [is that] it comes to nought and brings sin in its train." *Cf.* also pp. 129:2: "For thou shalt eat the labor of thine hand: Happy shalt thou be, and it shall be well with thee."

106. Enoch George Payne, *Principles of Educational Sociology,* p. 66, "The family of the child . . . is the most important group in giving social adjustment." See also Ernest O. Melby, "The Forward Look," *The Journal of Educational Sociology,* Vol. 24, No. 6, February 1951, p. 363, 367, "Schools alone cannot deal effectively with human relations problems . . . A feeling of security on the part of individual children and adults depends on [harmonious] human relationships in the home, school, and [the] community." See also the International Council of Religious Education, *Christian Education Today,* p. 20, "the primary and most intimate social group, the family, is potentially the most important means of Christian Education."

107. *Shulchan Aruch-Yoreh Deah,* 335:1.

108. *Ibid.,* 343:1.

109. *Ibid.,* 245:1.

110. *Shulchan Aruch-Orach Chayim,* 549:1. *Cf. ibid.,* 583:1, 670:1, and 687:1: "One should fast on the ninth day of the month of Ab to commemorate the destruction of the Temple; on the seventeenth of the month of Tamuz, the day when the Holy of Holies was defiled; and on the third day of Tishri [usually October] to commemorate the murder of Gedalyahu ben Achikam the last Jewish governor [appointed by Nebuchadnezzar, the King of Babylon, in 597 B.C.E.;] and on the tenth of Teveth [usually January], the day Nebuchadnezzar besieged Jerusalem." *Cf.* II *Kings,* 25:22, *et passim,* and Jeremiah 40:7 *et passim,* for the story of Gedaliahu ben Achikam.

111. *Exodus,* XX, 12. See also *Deuteronomy* V, 16.

112. *Shulchan Aruch-Yoreh Deah,* 240:1.

113. *Ibid.,* 240:2.

114. *Loc. cit.*

115. *Ibid.,* 240:4.

116. *Ibid.,* 240:3.

117. *Shulchan Aruch-Yoreh Deah,* 241:1.

118. *Ibid.,* 240:15. See also *ibid.,* 240:11, and 240;11. Compare *Leviticus* XIX, 3: "Ye

shall fear every man his mother and his father, and keep my Sabbaths," which is interpreted by Rashi to mean that children should not obey their parents when they command to desecrate the Sabbath. Note that the child is here charged with the responsibility to discern between obedience to God and obedience to parents.
119. *Ibid.*, 240:19. Compare *Maseket Derek Erez*, p. 40: "Be humble of spirit before all, especially before members of your family."
120. *Ibid.*, 240:21.
121. *Ibid.*, 240:24.
122. *Ibid.*, 240:22.
123. *Shulchan Aruch-Yoreh Deah*, 242:1.
124. *Ibid.*, 242:16.
125. *Loc. cit.*
126. *Ibid.*, 242:2.
127. *Ibid.*, 244:1.
128. *Shulchan Aruch-Choshen Mishpat*, 8, 9, and 10 *et passim*. Compare Exodus XVIII, 21–22, "Thou shalt provide out of all people able men, such as fear God, men of truth, hating covetousness... And let them judge the people." See also *Deuteronomy* XVI, 19–20.
129. E.V. Anderson, *Principles and Practices of Secondary Education*, p. 23, points out, among other principles: "A democratic society is characterized by an ever widening concern and responsibility for the welfare of others."
130. *Numbers* XI, 29.
131. *Shulchan Aruch-Orach Chayim*, 93:4. See also Arthur F. Corey, "Leadership in a Corporate Society," *Phi Delta Kappah*, Vol. 35 No. 7, April 1954, p. 259: "Leadership must be sincere and self-effacing." Note also Theodore Bienenstock, "Democratic Leadership and Fellowship in the School Program," *The Journal of Educational Sociology*, Vol. 27, No. 9, p. 407, May 1954: "The real desirable condition would be one in which a person would lead in those situations in which his knowledge, capacities, skill and vision justify this."
132. *Shulchan Aruch-Yoreh Deah*, 203:1.
133. *Ibid.*, 256:1. See also *Shulchan Aruch-Orach Chayim*, 576:16.
134. *Shulchan Aruch-Orach Chayim*, 525:2. See *Ibid.*, *Yoreh Deah*, 256:1.
135. *Shulchan Aruch-Yoreh Deah*, 244:6.
136. *Numbers*, XII:3. See also *ibid.*, *Yoreh Deah*.
137. *Shulchan Aruch-Choshen Mishpat*, 8:4. Compare Bienenstock, *op. cit.*, p. 401: "Simply putting premium on leadership... is often tantamount to putting a premium on aggressive urges toward dominance."
138. *Shulchan Aruch-Yoreh Deah*, 256:1, 2, and *ibid.*, *Choshen Mishpat*, 8:1.
139. *Shulchan Aruch-Choshen Mishpat*, 7:11. Compare also *Maseket Derek Erez*, pp. 33:1, 36:1, and 48:1.
140. *Shulchan Aruch-Yoreh Deah*, 214:2, and *Shulchan Aruch-Orach Chayim*, 263:12–13.
141. *Ibid.*, 228:34.
142. *Shulchan Aruch-Orach Chayim*, 574:5.
143. *Ibid.*, 53:19.

144. *Shulchan Aruch-Yoreh Deah*, 256:5. Compare *Maseket Derek Erez*, p. 108: "Concerning those who are merciful, who feed the hungry, who give drink to the thirsty, who clothe the naked, and distribute charity, the Scriptures say (*Isaiah* III:10), "Say ye of the righteous, that it shall be well with them." See also *ibid.*, pp. 108–109. Compare also *Ecclesiastes* XI:1: "Cast thy bread upon the waters: for thou shalt find it after many days." See also *Proverbs* X:12:: " . . . righteousness (charity) delivereth from death." Compare *Baba Bathra* 10a. Compare also WIlliam H. Fells, "Motivating Students for Civic Responsibilities," *Current Issues in Higher Education*, p. 108, March 1953: "[Motivation] may involve . . . working for a government office during the summer months, with or without pay."
145. *Shulchan Aruch-Yoreh Deah*, 246:1, and 247:4. Compare *Nedarim* 81a, *Seder Nashim*, Vol. V, p. 152: "Be heedful [not to neglect] the children of the poor, for from them Torah goes forth." Compare *Isaiah* LVIII:7.
146. *Shulchan Aruch-Yoreh Deah*, 256:1. Compare also *Shulchan Aruch-Orach Chayim* 576:16 where supervisors over public moral behavior are to be appointed.
147. *Ibid.*, 249:7.
148. *Ibid.*, 249:14.
149. *Ibid.*, 248:1.
150. *Loc. cit.*
151. *Shulchan Aruch-Yoreh Deah*, 247:1 and 247:4. Reference is to *Deuteronomy* XV:7.
152. Philip R.V. Curoe, *Principles of Education*, pp. 53–54, notes: "History should begin with the significance of holidays, with events and personages commemorated." But see John Dewey, *Democracy and Education*, p. 251: "The true starting point of history is always some present situation with its problems." It may be of interest to note here that H.W. Guenther in "Character Education is Everybody's Business," *Phi Delta Kappah*, Vol. XXXIV, No. 8, May 1953, p. 333, points out: "History and civics should stress loyalty and honesty."
153. Passover night meal. Lewis Joseph Sherrill, *The Rise of Christian Education*, p. 17 notes: "The Hebrew adults . . . took the most basic institution, the family, and made of it a 'school.' In the family-school they developed a body of ritual not surpassed in its richness."
154. *Shulchan Aruch-Orach Chayim*, 481:2.
155. A fast day commemorating the destruction of the Temple; usually falling in the corresponding month of July.
156. *Shulchan Aruch-Orach Chayim* 559:3.
157. *Ibid.*, 671:5.
158. *Ibid.*, 671:1.
159. *Ibid.*, 687:2.
160. *Shulchan Aruch-Yoreh Deah* 228:10. See also *ibid.*, 252:2. References are to *Leviticus* XIX:18, " . . . thou shalt love thy neighbor as thyself . . . " and to *Leviticus* XIX:16, 17, 23, 36, *Deuteronomy* XV, 7–8, and *Proverbs* XXIV:11.
161. *Ibid.*, 345:5.
162. See, for example, *Proverbs* XXII:6: "Train up a child in the way he should go: and when he is old, he will not depart from it."

163. Aboth II, 5, p. 15, *Nezikin*, Vol. VIII: "He [Hillel] used to say: an uncultured person is not sin-fearing, neither is an ignorant person pious."
164. *Shulchan Aruch-Yoreh Deah*, 246:26. Reference is to Aboth 4:11.
165. *Ibid.*, 246:7.
166. *Ibid.*, 246:8.
167. *Ibid.*, 245:11. Compare H.H. Horne, *The Psychological Principles of Education*, p. 347: "... religious education can never end."
168. See also *The Babylonian Talmud*, Yoma 35b, to the effect that when the poor man comes before 'Judgment' he is asked: "Why have you not occupied yourself with the Torah?... Were you poorer than Hillel?" (d. 10 C.E.) See also Yoma 28b for the importance of learning.
169. *Shulchan Aruch-Orach Chayim*, 334:12.
170. *Shulchan Aruch-Yoreh Deah*, 340:37.
171. *Ibid.*, 282:10.
172. *Shulchan Aruch-Orach Chayim*, 240:6.
173. *Shulchan Aruch-Yoreh Deah*, 242:1 and 20. Reference is to Aboth 4:16.
174. *Shulchan Aruch-Orach Chayim*, 472:13.
175. See, for instance, *Exodus* XII:49: "One law shall be to him that is home born, and to the stranger that sojourneth among you." Compare also *Leviticus* XIX:10, XXIII:22, *Numbers* XV:16, 29, *Deuteronomy* X:19, XXIII, 8, 9, and XXIV: 19–20. See also *Maseket Derek Erez*, p. 36: "Nine entered Paradise during their lives. [Among them were] Ebed-Melech, the Ethiopian King, Hiram, the King of Tyre ... and Bathiah, the daughter of Pharaoh."
176. *Shulchan Aruch-Orach Chayim*, 246:1.
177. *Ibid.*, 39:1. Reference is to *Deuteronomy* VI:8. See also *ibid.*, 14:1, relating to fringes.
178. *Shulchan Aruch-Choshen Mishpat*, 10:3.
179. *Shulchan Aruch-Choshen Mishpat*, 228:1 and 348:1. Compare *Deuteronomy* XXII, 1–4 and XXIV, 10–13.
180. *Ibid.*, 231:2. Reference is to *Leviticus* XIX, 35. Compare *Deuteronomy* XXV, 13–16.
181. *Ibid.*, 231:1.
182. *Shulchan Aruch-Orach Chayim*, 266:1. See also *ibid.*, 246:3, and *ibid.*, *Yoreh Deah*, 120:8. Reference is to *Exodus* XXIII, 12 and *Deuteronomy* 5:14.
183. *Shulchan Aruch-Yoreh Deah*, 244:7.
184. *Shulchan Aruch-Orach Chayim*, 576:3.
185. *Shulchan Aruch-Orach Chayim*, 224:7
186. *Ibid.*, 224:8. See also *ibid.*, 104:1 and 224:9.
187. *Shulchan Aruch-Choshen Mishpat*, 348:2.
188. *Shulchan Aruch-Yoreh Deah*, 69:10.
189. *Ibid.*, 320:2, 3, and 6. Reference is to *Numbers* 18:17.
190. *Jeremiah* XXIX, 7: "Seek ye the peace of the city whither I have caused you to be carried away captives, and pray unto the Lord for it; for in its welfare shall be peace." See also *Shulchan Aruch-Yoreh Deah*, 267:18 and 16. See also Aboth III, 2, p. 27, *Nezikin* Vol. VIII. "R. Ḥananiah, the Vice-High Priest, said: Pray ye for the welfare of the government, for were it not for the fear thereof, one man would

swallow up alive his fellow-man." *Cf.* also *Baba Kama*, 113a, pp. 663–86, *Seder Nezikin*, Vol. I.
191. *Shulchan Aruch-Yoreh Deah*, 334:48. See also *ibid.*, 334:18.
192. *Ibid.*, 334:44. See also *ibid.*, *Choshen Mishpat* 1:1, 26:1 *et passim*. Note that Rabbi L. Goldman, commenting on *Choshen Mishpat* 1:1 says: " . . . today the [Jewish] court has no such right and every lawsuit is to be contended in governmental courts."
193. *Shulchan Aruch-Choshen Mishpat*, 26:2.
194. *Shulchan Aruch-Orach Chayim*, 307:17.
195. *Ibid.*, 308:50.
196. *Shulchan Aruch-Yoreh Deah*, 246:4.
197. H.H. Horne, *The Psychological Principles of Education*, pp. 250 and 239.
198. *Shulchan Aruch-Orach Chayim*, 307:16. Reference is to *Leviticus* XIV:4 and Psalms 1:1. Compare Nathan Drazin, *History of Jewish Education*, p. 15: "Secular knowledge was brought to the child . . . in relation to the laws of permitted and forbidden foods, one learned directly and indirectly many facts of botany, zoology, physiology, anatomy, hygiene, and medicine. . . ." Compare also Aboth III, 18, pp. 41–42, *Nezikin*, Vol. VIII: "[The study of the] revolutions of the heavenly bodies and arithmetic are aftercourses of wisdom." See also *Nedarim*, 41a, pp. 129–130, *Seder Nashim*, Vol. VI: "Abaye said: We have a tradition that no one is poor save he who lacks knowledge. In the West [Palestine] there is a proverb: He who has this [knowledge] has everything; he who lacks this, what has he? Has one acquired this, what does he lack? Has he not acquired this, what does he possess?" See also *Yebamoth* II, p. 762, *Seder Nashim*, Vol. II: "R. Jose said: Whosoever says that he has only [an interest in the study of the] Torah . . . has no [reward] even [for the study of the] Torah."
199. *Shulchan Aruch-Yoreh Deah*, 245:5.
200. *Deuteronomy*, XXXIII, 4.
201. *Ibid.*, VI, 4–9.
202. "Sh'ma" means "hear" and refers to the affirmation of the unity of God. Note that in modern education, the pre-school environment "is to offer the child opportunities to learn but does not make demands for achievement." L. Joseph Stone and Joseph Church, *Childhood and Adolescence*, p. 193.
203. Referring to the twenty-five books of the Old Testament.
204. *Shulchan Aruch-Orach Chayim*, 245:6. *Cf.* 245, 4.
205. *Shulchan Aruch-Yoreh Deah*, 245:8. *Cf.* also 245:5 and Aboth V, 21, *Seder Nezikin*, Vol. VIII, pp. 74–75. Note that references to the Talmud in this thesis are to that of the Soncino Press.
206. *Shulchan Aruch-Yoreh Deah*, 245:8.
207. *Ibid.*, 245:11.
208. *Ibid.*, 245:12, 13, 14.
209. *Ibid.*, 245:10.
210. *Shulchan Aruch-Yoreh Deah*, 245:9. Neither the Shulchan Aruch nor the Talmud, *Baba Bathra* 21a, are explicit about whether the case is one of a slow learner or not. But the Talmud implies that as long as he reads along with other pupils, he is bound to learn.

211. *Shulchan Aruch-Yoreh Deah*, 246:10.
212. *Ibid.*, 246:21.
213. *Shulchan Aruch-Yoreh Deah*, 246:22.
214. See, for instance, *Provebs* XXVI, 6, "As is the one that bindeth a stone fast to a sling, so is he that giveth honor to a fool."
215. *Shulchan Aruch-Yoreh Deah*, 246:7.
216. *Deuteronomy* VI:7 and XI:19–20.
217. *Shulchan Aruch-Yoreh Deah*, 246:5.
218. *Shulchan Aruch-Yoreh Deah*, 245:20.
219. *Ibid.*, 245:21.
220. *Ibid.*, 245:22. Reference is to *Isaiah*, XLII:21.
221. *Shulchan Aruch-Yoreh Deah*, 245:18.
222. *Ibid.*, 245:19. *Cf.* also *ibid.*, 245:16.
223. *Ibid.*, 246:8.
224. *Shulchan Aruch-Yoreh Deah*, 245:17.
225. *Shulchan Aruch-Choshen Mishpat*, 334:4. *Cf. Ibid.*, 333:3 and 335:1.
226. *Ibid.*, 237:2.
227. *Shulchan Aruch-Yoreh Deah*, 248:5.
228. *Ibid.*, 246:4. *Cf. ibid.*, 246:2, 2 and 5.
229. *Shulchan Aruch-Yoreh Deah*, 246:6.

Chapter III

1. *Vide supra.* See Chapter II.
2. See, for instance, Philip W.L. Cox and Forrest E. Long, *Principles of Secondary Education,* p. 332, who note that modern progressive schools emphasize "pleasurable big-muscle activities." Herbert G. Lull, *Principles of Elementary Education,* pp. 457 ff., notes that traditional education did not accord physical education its proper place in the curriculum. Vernon E. Anderson, Paul H. Grimm and William T. Gruhn, *Principles and Practices of Secondary Education,* p. 157, complain that physical education has not yet reached "the prestige of other subjects."
3. See Chapter II of this thesis.
4. *Ibid.*
5. *Ibid.*
6. *Shulchan Aruch-Orach Chayim,* 3:2–4, 8–9, and 12–17.
7. See, for instance, Anderson, Grimm, and Gruhn, *op. cit.,* pp. 315–316, 476 *et passim. Cf.* Lull, *op. cit.,* p. 463.
8. See Chapter II.
9. See, for instance, Thomas M. Risk, *Principles and Practices of Teaching in Secondary Schools,* pp. 637 ff. *Cf.* Cox, *op. cit.,* p. 504. *Cf.* also John Dewey, *Democracy and Education,* p. 402.
10. See Chapter II, p. 55.
11. See, for instance, Anderson, Grimm, and Gruhn, *op. cit.,* pp. 141 ff.
12. See, for instance, Schorling, *op. cit.,* pp. 321, 325, 328.
13. See Chapter II.
14. Dewey, *op. cit.,* p. 198.
15. Anderson, Grimm, and Gruhn, *op. cit.,* pp. 230–35 *et passim. Cf.* Schorling, op. cit., pp. 183ff, 294 ff.
16. See Chapter II.
17. Vernon E. Anderson, Paul H. Grimm, and William T. Gruhn, *Principles and Practices of Secondary Education,* pp. 146ff., 152, 155ff. See, for instance Risk, *op. cit.,* pp. 353–357; *cf.* Herbert G. Lull, *Principles of Elementary Education,* pp. 182 and 190.
18. See Chapter II.
19. *Ibid.*
20. See Chapter II. *et passim. Cf.* J. Donald Butler, *Four Philosophies and their Practice in Education and Religion.* p. 372. *Cf.* Lull, *op. cit.,* pp. 652 ff. Schorling, *op. cit.,* p. 186 . . . See Chapter II.
21. See Chapter II.
22. *Ibid. CF.* Risk, *op. cit.,* pp. 157ff, 199ff, and 205ff, and Schorling, *op. cit.,* p. 186.

23. Raleigh Schorling, *Student Teaching*, pp. 232ff.
24. See Chapter II.
25. John Dewey, *Democracy and Education*, p. 418.
26. John S. Brubacher, *Modern Philosophies of Education, p. 332*. *Cf.* Paul Klapper, *Principles of Educational Practice*, p. 428.
27. See Chapter II.
28. Percival M. Symonds, *The Dynamics of Parent-Child Relationships*, pp. 116–123.
29. Robert J. Havighurst and Bernice L. Neugarten, *Society and Education*, pp. 66ff.
30. See Chapter II.
31. *Ibid.*
32. Thomas M. Risk, *Principles and Practices of Teaching in Secondary Schools*, p. 511, speaking of the teacher as a leader, notes that "pupils despise insincerity and lack of integrity."
33. See for instance, Anderson, Grimm and Gruhn, *op. cit.*, pp. 230ff.
34. See Chapter II.
35. See Chapter II. *Cf.* Butler, *op. cit.*, p. 418; Cox, *op. cit.*, pp. 218–219. *Cf.* Anderson, Grimm, and Gruhn, *op. cit.*, pp. 162–63, 224, and pp. 239–262.
36. See Chapter II. where the uninterrupted study of the Torah is advocated in order to maintain the religious spirit.
37. See John Dewey, *Democracy and Education*, pp. 250–255. *Cf.* Anderson, Grimm and Gruhn, *op. cit.*, pp. 146ff, 162–168, 153–155, and 172–174.
38. See Chapter II.
39. See, for instance, Dewey, *op. cit.*, pp. 100ff. *Cf.* Anderson, Grimm, and Gruhn, *op. cit.*, pp. 28ff. *Cf.* Schorling, *op. cit.*, pp. 341–342.
40. See Chapter II. *Cf.*, *Shulchan Aruch-Choshen Mishpat*, 369:6 *et passim*.
41. See, for instance, Anderson, Grimm, and Gruhn, *op. cit.*, pp. 230ff.
42. See Chapter II.
43. See, for instance, *Shulchan Aruch-Orach Chayim*, 4:1, and Chapter II. of this thesis.
44. *Shulchan Aruch-orach Chayim*, 634:1.
45. *Ibid.*, 62:1 *et passim*.
46. *Shulchan Aruch-Yoreh Deah*, 31:1 *et passim*.
47. See, for instance, Dewey, *op. cit.*, p. 417.
48. See Chapter II.
49. *Ibid.*
50. See, for instance, Ruth Strang, *Introduction to Child Study*, p. 277.
51. See, for instance, *ibid.*, p. 175.
52. See Chapter II.
53. See, for instance, Vernon E. Anderson, Paul H. Grimm, and William T. Gruhn, *Principles and Practices of Secondary Education*, pp. 75–76 *et passim*. *Cf.* Schorling, *op. cit.*, pp. 208–210. *Cf.* Dewey, *op. cit.*, pp. 226 *et passim*.
54. See Chapter II of this thesis.
55. See, for instance, this chapter *et passim*.
56. *Shulchan Aruch-Yoreh Deah*, 245;12–15.

57. See, for instance, Anderson, who favors very small classes. *Cf.* Anderson, Grimm, and Gruhn, *op. cit.*, pp. 375–376, also Philip W.L. Cox and Forrest E. Long, *Principles of Secondary Education*, p. 8. *Cf.* Herbert G. Lull, *Principles of Elementary Education*, pp. 131–132, where he urges a small number of students where invidividual attention is required.
58. See Chapter II of this thesis.
59. Thomas M. Risk, *Principles and Practices of Teaching in Secondary Schools*, p. 703. *Cf.* Dewey, *op. cit.*, pp. 161–162; *cf. Raleigh Schorling, Student Teaching*, pp. 90–92.
60. See Chapter II of this thesis. *Cf. Shulchan Aruch-Yoreh Deah*, 245:10.
61. See, for instance, Ruth Strang, *Introduction to Child Study*, p. 342. *Cf.* Anderson, Grimm, and Gruhn, *op. cit.*, pp. 143 and 402. *Cf.*, Schorling, *op. cit.*, pp. 186–187. *Cf.* "Curriculum Development in the Elementary Schools," *Curriculum Bulletin* Number 1, 1955–56, p. 2.
62. John Dewey, *Democracy and Education* pp. 353-354.
63. Lull, *op. cit.*, pp. 85ff.
64. See Chapter II of this thesis.
65. See, for instance, Risk, *op. cit.*, pp. 532-533. *Cf.* Cox and Long, pp. 417ff.
66. See Chapter II of this thesis.
67. See, for instance, Charles H. Handschin, *Modern-Language Teaching*, pp. 79, 109, 194-196. *Cf.*, Risk, *op. cit.*, pp. 371ff. *Cf.*, Schorling, *op. cit.*, pp. 201-204. *Cf.*; Lull, *op. cit.*, 371ff, and Cox and Long, *op. cit.*, pp. 387ff.
68. See Chapter II of this thesis.
69. Handschin, *op. cit.*, p. 198.
70. See Chapter II of this thesis.
71. See Chapter II of this thesis.
72. See, for instance, Robert J. Havighurst and Bernice L. Neugarten, *Society and Education*, pp. 406-410 *et passim*. *Cf.*, Edward G. Olsen, *School and Community*, pp. 268 *et passim*. *Cf.*, Andersen, Orimm, and Ornhn, *op. cit.*, pp. 468ff. *Cf.*, J. Donald Butler, *Four Philosophies and their Practice in Education and Religion*, pp. 240-243; Cox and Long, *op. cit.*, pp. 424ff and 557 ff; also Lull, *op. cit.*, pp. 12ff. *et passim*.
73. See Chapter II of this thesis; *Shulchan Aruch-Yoreh Deah*, 246:8.
74. The Society for Curriculum Study, *An Evaluation of Modern Education*, p. 133. Of interest is the following quotation by the Educational Policies Commission, National Education Association of the United States and the American Association of School Administration, *Moral and Spiritual Values in the Public Schools*, April 1964, p. 55; "Since the ultimate success of a program to develop moral and spiritual values depends largely on the teacher, the institutions which educate teachers should give full recognition to these values in their curricula. . . . Personal character of an acceptable quality to serve as an example to American youth often determines the success or failure of a teacher in teaching subject matter as well as in contributing to moral development. Character, therefore, should invariably be an important consideration in the employment of a teacher. The education institutions should consider character along with scholarship and teaching skills, in the selection of students, in judging the competence of student teachers, and in the

recommendation of prospective teachers to boards of education." *Cf.* Risk, *op. dt.*, pp. 509-511, and Havighurst and Neugarten, *op. cit.*, pp. 390 and 394, for different ways in which the teacher may exert influence upon pupils.
75. See Chapter II of this thesis.
76. See, for instance, Vernon E. Anderson, Paul H. Grimm, and William T. Gruhn, *Principles and Practices of Secondary Education*, pp. 239-240 *et passim*. *Cf.* Herbert G. Lull, *Principles of Elementary Education*, pp. 507ff; also Philip W.L. Cox and Forrest E. Long, *Principles of Secondary Education*, pp. 560ff.
77. See Chapter II of this thesis.
78. See, for instance, Isidore Fishman, *The History of Jewish Education in Central Europe from the End of the Sixteenth to the End of the Eighteenth Century*, pp. 118-121.

Chapter IV

1. Joseph Caro, Introduction, *Arba Turim-Tur Orach Chayim* by Rabenu Yaacov ben Rabenu Asher. To this work Caro appended his famous commentary, *The Beth Yosef*, which was the basis for the Shulchan Aruch (see Chapter I).
2. Gemara or *Talmud* consists of the *Mishnah* and its commentators, and serves as an interpretation of the Torah.
3. *Tur...op. cit.*, note #1 above.
4. Initials of Rabenu Itzchak al-Fasi (1013-1103), known for his *Hallachoth* or *Hilchoth Rav Alfas*, a compendium of legal decisions of the Talmud.
5. Initials of Rabenu Mosheh ben Maimon (Maimonides) (1135-1204), famous for his work, the *Yad Hachazakah*.
6. Initials of Rabenu Asher ben Yechiel (1250-1328), famous for his work, *Piskay Ha-Rash* which served as a basic for the *Arba Turim* of Asher (see Note #1 on previous page).
7. Initials of Rabenu Mosheh ben Nachman Gerondi (Nachmanides) (1194-1270).
8. Initials of Rabenu Shelomo ben Abraham Adret (1235-1310).
9. Initials of Rabenu Nissim (ben Rabenu Gerondi) (ca. 1340-1380).
10. Whose full name is Mordecai ben Hillel Ashkenazi (d. 1928).
11. Initials of a work entitled *Sefer Mitzvoth Gedoloth* whose author, Rabbi Mosheh ben Yaacov of Couci, known for short as the Ra'M, lived in the first half of the thirteenth century.
12. Rabbi Shelomo Zalman of Volozhin, known as Rabbi Zalmelo of Vilna, states that the source is in *Yad Hachazakah*, Book II, part 3, Chapter II,11. See *HaBrez HaVilna*, p. 54.
13. Caro, *op. cit.*, Introduction, *Tur Orach Chayim*, Part I.
14. See, for instance, Shimon Hones, *Sefer Toledoth Haposekim*, p. 573.
15. The list of additional sources are appended at the end of this chapter.
16. Introduction, *Tur Orach Chayim*, free translation.
17. Reference is to *Leviticus* XI;43, XX;25.
18. *Shulchan Aruch-Orach Chayim*, 3;17.
19. Reference is to *Exodus* XXIII;8.
20. Reference is to *Leviticus* XIX;14.
21. *Shulchan Aruch-Chosen Mishpat*, 9;1.
22. Reference is to *Numbers* XV;38-39.
23. *Shulchan Aruch-Orach Chayim* 24;6. Cf. *Menaḥoth* 43b.
24. Reference is to *Deuteronomy* VI;8-9.
25. *Shulchan Aruch-Orach Chayim*, 25:5.
26. Reference is to *Deuteronomy* XV;7 et passim.
27. *Shulchan Aruch-Yoreh Deah*, 247;1. Cf. *Baba Bathra* 10a.

28. Reference is to *Exodus* XX;13.
29. *Shulchan Aruch-Chosen Mishpat*, 348;1-2. *Cf.Shulchan Aruch-Orach Chayim*, 17;1 and 625;1, with reference to *Numbers* XV;39 and *Leviticus* XXIII;43, respectively. Also *Shulchan Aruch-Orach Chayim*, 9;1, 25;5, and 58;3. See also *Raba Kama* 113b. Note that social justice is here stressed to people of other religions.
30. *Shulchan Aruch-Orach Chayim* 1;1. *Cf. Tur, op. cit.*, reference is to Aboth V;23.
31. *Shulchan Aruch-Orach Chayim*, 2;2. *Cf. Tagnith* 11a.
32. *Ibid.*, 89;2. *Cf. Brachoth* 14a with reference to *Isaiah* II;22.
33. *Ibid.*, 93;1. *Cf. Brachoth* 30b with reference to *I Samuel*, 1;10, *Psalma* V;8, etc.
34. The words *Kesef Mishnah* may be rendered as meaning "double silver" (money). However, Caro states that he uses these words to express his own strong yearning—and that of others—to understand Maimonides' work. See Joseph Caro, Introduction, *Yad Hachazakah*, Vol. I.
35. In the Introduction to the *Yad Hachazakah*, Caro expresses himself about Maimonides' style as being concise and lucid.
36. See, for instance, p. 131, comparative passage, line 1, where Caro uses the phrase—"Just as one is commanded" while Maimonides uses the term "obligated". The two terms are quite synonymous.
37. For instance, "26:1" means paragraph 26, subparagraph 1. Note that Rabbi Jacob ben Asher in his *Arba Turim* numbers only the paragraphs.
38. See p. 131, second comparative passages, first line.
39. *Baba Bathra* 21a.
40. *Shabbath*, 119b.
41. In his index, known as the *Be'er HaGolah*
42. *Kesef Mishneh* on *Yad Hachazakah*, Book I, Part III, Chapter 2;1.
43. See p. 135, second comparative passage.
44. See p. 135, second comparative passage.
45. *Shulchan Aruch-Yoreh Deah*, 245:7. Note that Rabbi Moses Rivkash, in his *Be'er HaGolah*, indexing Caro's sources, points out Maimonides' *Yad Hachazakah*.
46. *Yad Hachazakah*, Book I, Part III, 2:1. *Cf. Baba Bathra* 21a and *Deuteronomy* XI:19. Note that Caro in his commentary *Kesef Mishnah* remarks that Maimonides maintained both Talmudic versions, namely *excommunicated* and *banned*, thus indicating that his own version and decision are to be found in Maimonides' code.
47. All the quotations from the Talmud are from the Soncino translation.
48. High Priest, officiated about 64 C.E.
49. *Baba Bathra* 21, Vol III, part 1, p. 106.
50. Palestinian scholar (200-275).
51. Lived at Tiberias in the middle of the third century.
52. Babylonian scholar, died about 420.
53. *Shabbath* 119b, Vol. 11, Part 2, p. 591.
54. *Tur Yorah Deah*, 245. Joseph Caro in his *Beth Yosef*, commenting on the *Tur* that the author incorporated the two Talmudic expressions (*excommunicated* and *banned*) as did Maimonides.
55. *Shulchan Aruch-Yoreh Deah*, 245;2. Compare *Kiddushin* XXIXb. Rabbi Moses Rivkash, in *B'er HaGolah*, in his index of sources, points out that the last part of

the passage is the same as that of Maimonides; while the rest is from the Talmud, *Kiddushin* 29b.
56. *Yad Hachazakah*, Book 1, Part III, 1:4. Joseph Caro, in his *Kesef Mishnah*, commenting on Maimonides' ruling, notes that he uses the expression—"Even so he should not cease learning"—in order to let us know that even though the father might have to support his son while the son studies the Torah, nevertheless, this does not relieve the father from the duty of studying the Torah himself. For these, Caro points out, are two separate commandments, which the father is responsible for fulfilling. We also note that Caro uses in the first line of his ruling the words—"He needed to study"—while Maimonides uses the words—"He *wanted* to study." (Italics mine)
57. *Kiddushin*, 29b, Vol. VIII, p. 141.
58. *Tur Yoreh Deah*, 245. Caro, in his *Beth Yosef*, commenting on the *Tur*, notes that the ruling is that of Maimonides who in turn decides like Rabbi Judah in the Talmud (*Kiddushi*, 29b).
59. *Kiddushin*, 29b. Note that the RA'SH quotes from the Talmud, except that he adds the words "and this is the law."
60. Reference is to *Joshua*, I:8.
61. *Shulchan Aruch-Yoreh Deah*, 246:1. Rabbi Moses Rivkash, in *Be'er HaGolah* notes that the version is that of Maimonides, while the Talmudic sources he indicates as *Baba Metzia*, 84b; *Ta'anith*, 25a; *Berachoth*, 28a; *Yoma*, 35b; and *Kethuboth*, 105a.
62. Reference is to *Joshua*, I;8.
63. *Yad Hachazakah*, Book I, Part III, 1:8. Joseph Caro, in his *Kesef Mishnah*, commenting on Maimonides' sources, states that in the Talmud there are many examples of sages who were sick and poor and that all of them did yet busy themselves studying the Torah.
64. A great scholar, lived ca. 30 B.C.E.—10 C.E.
65. Lived in second century (see J.E. "Severus").
66. Reference to *Genesis* XXXIX, 10.
67. *Yoma*, 35b, Vol. V, pp. 163-164. *Cf. Taanith*, 25a, *Peaachim*, 116b, *Kethuboth*, 105a, *Baba Matzia*, 84b, and *Berachoth*, 28a for other Talmudic scholars who were either sick, blind, manual laborers, or studying at great inconvenience.
68. Reference is to *Joshua* I:8.
69. *Tur Yoreh Deah*, 246. Caro, in his *Beth Yosef*, commenting on the *Tur*, notes that the version is that of Maimonides, as is also the decision. Thus, even the *Tur* may be said to have been influenced by Maimonides.
70. Reference is to *Deuteronomy* XI:19.
71. *Shulchan Aruch-Yoreh Deah*, 245:3. Reference is to *Kiddushin*, 30a. Rabbi Moses Rivkash, in his *Be'er HaGolah*, indicates that the first half of Caro's version is found in the Talmud, *Kiddushin*, 30a, while the second half is that of Maimonides.
72. Reference is to *Deuteronomy* XI:19.
73. *Yad Hachazakah*, Book I, Part III, 1:2.
74. Reference is to *Deuteronomy* XI, 19.
75. *Ibid.*, IV, 9.
76. *Kiddushin* 30a, Vol. VIII, p. 143.

77. Reference is to *Deuteronomy* IV:9.
78. *Tur Yoreh Deah*, 245. Caro, in his *Beth Yosef*, commenting on the *Tur*, indicates that the last part of the version is entirely that of Maimonides. We note, on p. 100, that Caro himself uses the same version. And on this same page, note 6, we observed that Caro indicated the source of Maimonides' ruling in the Talmud. Here, however, Caro points out that the version is that of Maimonides.
79. RiF on *Kiddushin*, 30a. Note that the RiF quotes the Talmud to a great extent.
80. *Shulchan Aruch-Yoreh Deah*, 249:3. *Cf. Baba Bathra*, 9a.
81. *Yad Hachazakah*, Book VIII, Part 2, 10:4.
82. The Hebrew is literally "evil eye".
83. *Shulchan Aruch-Yoreh Deah*, 249:1. Rabbi Moses Rivkash, in his *B'er HaGolah*, indicates that the version is that of Maimonides, and that the Talmudic sources are *Kethuboth*, 50a and 67b.
84. The Hebrew term would mean "befittingly" and refers to the needs of the poor commensurate with his status.
85. Same as Note #5 on preceding page.
86. *Yad Hachazakah*, Book VII, Part 2, 7:1,5. Joseph Caro, in his commentary *Kesef Mishneh*, remarks that the amount of charity to be given, as is indicated in Maimonides' ruling, refers only to a lving person, while the Talmud (*Kethuboth*, 67b) indicates that one may leave in his will any amount. From this remark by Caro, we may conclude that in his own decision he relied also on the Talmud.
87. *Kethuboth*, 50a, Vol. III, Part 1, p. 286. *Cf. ibid.*, 67b.
88. *Tur Orach Chayim*, 249. The Hebrew term is literally "evil eye." Joseph Caro, in his commentary *Beth Yosef*, remarks that "It is apparent that 'our Master' [referring to Rabenu Ya'acov, the codifier of the *Tur*] is influenced by [literally: "is drawn after"] the version of Maimonides."
89. *Baba Bathra*, 9a, Vol. III, Part 1, p. 41.
90. *Shabbath*, 151b, Vol. II, Part 2, p. 774.
91. Reference is to *Isaiah*, 32:17.
92. *Tur Yoreh Deah*, 247.
93. *Kethuboth* 50a. Note that the wording is identical with that of the Talmud.
94. SeMa'G, *Mitzvoth Asseh*, 162.
95. *Shulchan Aruch-Orach Chayim*, 246:1, *Cf. Exodus* XX, 8-12 and *Deuteronomy* V, 12-16.
96. *Yad Hachazakah*, Book III, Part 1, 6:16.
97. School of Shammai.
98. School of Hillel.
99. *Shabbath*, 17b, Vol. I, Part 1, p. 73.
100. *Ibid.*, 18b, p. 77 *Cf. ibid.*, 19a.
101. *Tur Orach Chayim*, 246.
102. *Shabbath*, 19a.
103. *Yoma*, 84b.
104. *Ibid.*
105. Mordechai, on *Sabbath*, 17a.
106. *Shulchan Aruch-Orach Chayim*, 328:2.
107. *Shulchan Aruch-Orach Chayim*, 328:12.

108. *Yad Hachazakah*, Book III, Part 1, 2:1, 3.
109. *Yoma*, 83a, Vol. V, p. 407.
110. *Ibid.*, 84b, p. 416.
111. *Shabbath*, 109a, p. 416. *Cf. ibid.*, 18a.
112. *Yoma*, 84b, Vol. II, Part 2, p. 530.
113. *Tur Orach Chayim*, 328.

CHAPTER V

1. Chapter I.
2. Chapter II.
3. Chapter III.
4. Chapter IV.
5. It may be of interest to note here that Dr. William W. Brickman, in his article, "A Visit to Soviet Jewry," Jewish Life, February 1958, pp. 8-19, states (on pp. 16-17): "In spite of several attempts on my part to arouse interest in the Jewish education of children, the Jews in the synagogues avoided any discussion of this painful subject. . . . The Chief Rabbi reminded me of the fact that more than a year ago, Professor Abraham I. Katsch, New York Univesity, had obtained a written promise from the Russian Republic's Ministry of Education to the effect that Hebrew or Yiddish would be taught in any school, provided the parents made the request. I was told that no ten parents could be found to express themselves in favor of Hebrew education." Professor Brickman's conclusion is significant: "To me it is obvious that no ten parents feel that they *dare* make such a request."
6. Simcha Asaf, *Mekoroth Letoledoth Hachinuch BeIsrael*, (Sources of the History of Jewish Education), Vol. I, p. 43 and note # 3, quoting Rabbi Chayim ben Bezalel (d. 1855) from the Introduction to his work, *Beer Mayim Chayim*, 1575 approximately; see *Shem Hagdolim-Berachoth Sefarim*, p. 19a.
7. When referring to Poland in this discussion, this writer has in mind not merely the political area of the present Polish State, but also its environs. Present Polish territory, though held at one time or another by other powers, would be considered as Polish for our purpose. This approach seems practical as the Shulchan Aruch was not adopted formally by any one country *per se* but by individual communities within a general area. Thus, Jews living in Lithuanian cities bordering on Poland, or in German cities on the Polish boundary, who follow the Shulchan Aruch, will in our study be regarded as Polish.
8. The number of lands participating in this Council varied from five to three. The Council lasted from the middle of the sixteenth century to the middle of the eighteenth century. *Cf.*, Dubnow, *the History of the Jews in Russia and Poland*, I:109-113; *Cf.*, Duchow, "Council of Four Lands," *Jewish Encyclopedia*, IV:304-308.
9. Great Poland's capital was then Posen. See Dubnow, *The History of the Jews in Russia and Poland*, I-110.
10. Little Poland was represented by the communities of Cracow and Lublin. See Dubnow, *loc. cit.*
11. Red or Polish Russia's capital was Lemberg. See Dubnow, *loc. cit.*
12. Volhynia's representative communities were Ostrog and Kremenetz. *Loc. cit.*

13. Lithuania was represented by its communities of Brest and Grodno. We note that some names of the communities mentioned in the preceding note very slightly in Budnow's article in the *Jewish Encyclopedia*, IV:304-308.
14. Israel Halpern, *Pinkas Vaad Arba Aratzoth*, p. 34. *Cf., Shulchan Aruch-Orach Chayim*, 61:6, 7,14-24, for some rules of grammar.
15. Halpern, *op. cit.*, pp. 96-97.
16. Moses Isserles is the rabbi whose emendations made the Shulchan Aruch the authoritative code for Polish Jewry. Cf. Chapter I of this thesis.
17. Rabbi Mosheh Rivkash or "Rivkes", meaning the son of Rivkah or Rebecca, d. 1671 or 1672. The title under which the sources are indicated is *Beer Hagolah*.
18. Halpern, *op. cit.*, p. 273.
19. *Ibid.*, p. 240.
20. Halbern, *op. cit.*, pp. 497-98. The Hebrew term is "*she'Halachah Kemotho*" and means literally "that according to it [the Shulchan Aruch] is the law."
21. Known as *Mishnah Berurah*, so named after his commentary on the *Shulchan Aruch-Orach Chayyim*.
22. Reference is to *Leviticus*, XVIII, 5.
23. See Introduction, *Mishnah Berurah*, pp. 5-6; free translation.
24. Part I.
25. Rabbi Moses Isserles, Introduction to *Shulchan Aruch-Choshen Mishpat*.
26. Aaron Sversky, Introduction to *Maggid Maysharim*, p. 8.
27. S. M. Dubnow, *History of the Jews in Russia and Poland*, Vol. I, p. 130.
28. H. Graetz, *History of the Jews*, Vol. IV, p. 613.
29. Most of the information concerning the Shulchan Aruch as a subject of study in Jewish educational institutions, especially in Europe, is not based on curricula; for while in every Yeshivah and in every rabbinical seminary the Shulchan Aruch has been an integral part of the curriculum, studied together with the Talmud, these institutions have not adopted the custom of publishing their curricula. *Cf.* Appendix, p. 40.
30. Joseph Caro, Introduction, *Shulchan Aruch-Orach Chayim*, also Introduction, *Shulchan Aruch-Choshen Mishpat*, Part I.
31. Louis Greenberg, *The Jews in Russia*, Vol. I, pp. 61-62, states that the standard guide for the Jews of Russia was the *Shulchan Aruch*. This Code, the universal guide for all Jewry of pre-emancipation days, regulated to the minutest detail every act of the Jew.
32. Simcha Asaf, *Mekoroth Letoledoth Hachinuch BeIsrael*, Vol. I, Introduction, p. X.
33. Rabbi Nathan Nata Hanover (d. 1663), *Even Metzulah*, (Venice, 1653). This work is a history of the Jews of Poland and the Ukraine during the years 1648-1649. *Cf.* Asaf, *op. cit.*, pp. 110-112.
34. Rabbi Chayim Chanz, *Responsa Divray Chayim*, Part X, Paragraph 47; referred to in Asaf, *op. cit.*, Vol. IV, pp. 210-211.
35. Rabbi Zelig ben Rabbi Itzchak Isaak, Introduction, *Hibburey Likutim*, Venice, 1715. Referred to in Asaf, *op. cit.*, Vol. I, pp. 165-169.
36. Rabbi Pinchas ben Rabbi Yehudah, *Rosh Hagiv'a (Vilna, 1898). Referred to in*

Asaf, op. cit., Vol. I, pp. 268-270. The Hebrew term "La'Asoth" meaning "to do" means in this context "to teach."

37. Asaf, *op. cit.,* Vol. I, p. 270 (free translation).
38. Yehudah Yudel Halevi Epstein, Introduction, *Minhat Yahudah,* (Warsaw, 1897). *Cf.* Asaf, *op. cit.,* Vol. IV, pp. 179-180.
39. Asaf, *op. cit.,* Vol. IV, pp. 167-169.
40. Rabbi Chayim Volozhin, *Orchoth Chayim,* printed as an addendum to *Siddur Hagr'o* (Jerusalem, 1935). *Cf.* Asaf, *op. cit.,* Vol. IV, p. 163.
41. Full name is Shabbathai Sheftel Horowitz. Lived in the sixteenth and seventeenth centuries, d. 1660. Also chief rabbi of Frankfort; referred to in Asaf, *op. cit.,* Vol. I, pp. 68-70.
42. "Ashrey" refers to Psalm CXLV which is recited three times daily during prayers, twice in the morning and once in the evening, and is therefore well known.
43. Rabbi Ya'acov of Lisa, d. 1832. Referred to in Asaf, *op. cit.,* Vol. I, pp. 272-273.
44. Rabbi Yosef ben Meir, introductory notes to *Peri Megadim,* (Frankfort on the Oder, 1787), reprinted and appended to *Shulchan Aruch-Orach Chayim,* Part I. Free translation.
45. See note #4 on preceding page.
46. Isidore Fishman points out that the study of the Shulchan Aruch was a requirement for the degree of Morenu ("Our Master"). This title signified that its recipient was an ordained rabbi and a scholar. *The History of Jewish Education in Central Europe from the End of the Sixteenth to the End of the Eighteenth Century,* pp. 29-31.
47. Shabbathai Meshorer Bas, Introduction, *Sifthey Yeshaynim,* (Amsterdam, 1680). *Cf.* Asaf, *op. cit.,* Vol. I, pp. 155-156.
48. Jacob R. Marcus, *The Jew in the Medieval World, a Source Book, 315-1791,* points out that the translation was into Spanish. In the original document, however, quoted by Asaf, *op. cit.,* Vol. I, pp. 155-156, Spanish is not mentioned.
49. Asaf, *op. cit.,* Vol. I, pp. 155-156.
50. Marcus, *op. cit.,* p. 200.
51. *Quellenschriften zur Geschichte des Unterrichts und der Erziung bei den deutschen Juden,* Vol. IV, p. 73.
52. Simcha Asaf, *Mekoroth Letoledoth Hachinuch BeIsrael,* Vol. I, p. 177.
53. As quoted in Asaf, *op. cit.,* Vol. I, pp. 178-181.
54. Who, after conversion to Christianity, was called Julio Morosini, (1612-1687).
55. In his work, *Via della Fedo* (Rome 1683); as quoted in Asaf, *op. cit.,* Vol. II, pp. 133-135.
56. The sections dealing with the Shulchan Aruch as well as the various regulations are discussed fully by Asaf, *op. cit.,* Vol. II, pp. 169-182. Reference to the Shulchan Aruch is on pp. 174-175.
57. Three different copies of rules of the Talmud Torah are discussed by Asaf, in addition to two copies of curriculum programs. Cf. Asaf, *op. cit.,* Vol. II, pp. 141-146.
58. These rules are discussed fully by Asaf, *op. cit.,* Vol. II, pp. 206-213. Reference to the teaching of the Shulchan Aruch is on pp. 210-211.

59. These regulations are discussed by Asaf, *op cit.*, Vol. II, pp. 182-197. The paragraph concerned with the teaching of the Shulchan Aruch is on p. 186.
60. Wetzler, in his *Liebes Brief* (manuscript form, written in Cella, Germany, 1749) referred to in Asaf, *op. cit.*, Vol. IV, pp. 111-119. It is interesting to note that Wetzler complains that in his time the Jewish youth in Germany did not know enough of the Shulchan Aruch to be called worthy Jews. (Asaf, *op. cit.*, p. 114); he further points out that a number of Jews learn the *Shulchan Aruch-Choshen Mishpat*, dealing with legal procedures in court cases, so as to appear like judges to the layman (Asaf, *op. cit.*, p. 116). Wetzler advises that whenever possible the youth should be taught those Talmudic tractates which deal with the laws of the *Shulchan Aruch-Orach Chayim* and Yoreh Deah, the first and the second parts respectively. (Asaf, *op. cit.*, p. 118.)
61. Friedlander's letter was published by Yosef Misel in *Historische Shriften*, YIVO, II, 394-412. Referred to by Asaf, *op. cit.*, Vol. IV, pp. 193-196. As in the preceding case, this writer complains about the lack of interest among Jewish youth in Germany with regard to Jewish education: "Not even the Humash [Pentateuch] and the Shulchan Aruch" is studied. (As quoted in Asaf, *op. cit.*, p. 118.)
62. Chayim Bachrach, *Sefer Sh'Eloth Uteshuvoth Havath Yair*, responsa 148, pp. 144-146, (Frankfurt o/M, 1699). Information about the status of Jewish education in Germany is found in Mordechai Eliav, "Hachinuch Hayehudi BeGermaniah Bimay HaHaskalah Vehaemantzipatziah" (Jewish Education in Germany during the Period of Enlightenment and Emancipation"), *Hagaoth Hasefarim shel Ha-Sochnuth Hayehudith l'Eretz Israel*. *Cf.* Samson Raphaelson Hirsch, *The Nineteen Letters of Ben Uziel*, (translated from the German *Neunzehn Briefe Uber Judenthum von Ben Uziel*, by Bernard Drachman).
63. Rabbi Itzchak Molcho, *Orchoth Yosher*, as quoted by Asaf, *op. cit.*, Vol. III, pp. 74-75.
64. Often, the fact that a work is reprinted may indicate its importance. In the case of the Shulchan Aruch, it was noted in previous pages, the Council of Four Lands deemed it important to print both the Code and prayer books that were edited according to its rules. (Some of the various reprints are listed in the bibliography at the end of this thesis.)
65. Jacob Shatzky, *Yiddishe Bildungs Politik in Poiln fun 1806 bis 1886*, (Jewish Educational Policies in Poland between 1806-1866), p. 146.
66. *Ibid.*, p. 165. Neufeld's original document in Polish is on pp. 251-258. It may be of itnerest to note that he felt that elementary schools for girls should be maintained by the Jewish community. See also, *ibid.*, p. 186.
67. Miriam Eisenstein, *Jewish Schools in Poland*, 1919-1939, p. 88. Note that Shelomo Zalman Kahane, "Mifalah HaChinuchi shel Hayahaduth HaDithith BePolin" in *Hachinuh Vehatarbuth Hayivrith B'Eyropah* states that the Yavnah institutions were established in 1930.
68. Eisenstein, *op. cit.*, p. 90.
69. Kahane, *op. cit.*, pp. 93, 99 (see note #1, above).
70. The Mizrachi schools have been teaching the Shulchan Aruch in all their schools in Europe, Israel, and the United States, from the Elementary up through the rabbinical seminaries. The only difference was that in the lower classes of the elementary

schools the laws contained in the Shulchan Aruch were taught orally; as the students progressed up in their Hebrew studies, from the fifth year up to the graduation of the elmentary schools, textbooks containing extracts and digests of the Shulchan Aruch were used. A list of some of these books will be appended at the end of this thesis.

71. The yeshivah was established in Minsk, Russia, in 1896 by Rabbi Yosef Yosel, and branched out over different parts of Russia. Later, about 1919, during the civil war in Russia, branches were established also in Poland. In 1929, several units of the Yeshivoth were opened in Palestine, and in 1930, in Latvia. The Yeshivah also has units in France and the United States.
72. Yehudah Leib Nakritz, "Yeshivoth Novardok" (The title in English is rendered as "Yeshivath Bait Josef of Novardok".) *Mosedoth Torah B'Eyropah BeVinyanam Ub'Churbanam*, p. 281. (See Section B, sub-paragraph *a*.)
73. Nakritz, *op. cit.*, p. 277.
74. Yosef Fridenson, "Garesheth HaChinuchith shel Agudath Israel, BePolin," *HaChinuch VeHaTarbuth Hayivrith B'Europah bein Shetei Milchamoth HaOlam*, p. 43. Its first cheder was organized in 1916. (p. 44)
75. *Ibid.*, p. 46.
76. Eisenstein, *Jewish Schools in Poland, 1919-1939*, pp. 71-72, lists among the most famous orthodox yeshivoth in Poland the ones of Mir, Baranowicze, Bialystok, Vilna, Brest-Litovsk, Lomza, Lublin, Otwock, Pinsk, Radin, Rowne, Slonim, Kleck, Grodno, Kamenac, and Warsaw. In Warsaw, there were five yeshivoth, the Mesivta, Emek Halachah, Tomchei Tmimim, Torath Chayim, and Beth Jacob. (p. 74)
77. Eisenstein, *op. cit.*, p. 79. It may be of interest to note here the numerical breakdown of the various religious schools in Poland in 1938 as follows: Mizrachi-Yavneh schools, 229; Chorev schools, 177; Chorev-Vilno schools, 190; Yeshivoth, 103; Vaad Hayeshivoth, 103; Vaad Hayeshivoth schools, 64; and Beth Jacob schools, 248. *Cf.*, "Notes and News," *Jewish Education*, Vol. X, no. 1, January-March 1938, p. 60.
78. The program was formulated by Rabbi Yeshudah Leib Orlean. This program served also as a basis for the Beth Yaacov schools for girls in Israel. *Cf.* Desler, *op. cit.*, Appendix, pp. 1-3
79. Desler, *Tochnith Halimudim*, 1959, Beith Chinuch Hayivri, Appendix, pp. 1-3.
80. Desser, *op. cit.*, p. 3.
81. *Loc. cit.*
82. *Loc. cit.*
83. Desser, *op. cit.*, p. 3.
84. *Shulchan Aruch-Orach Chayim*, 251:1.
85. Desser, *op. cit.*, p. 3.
86. *Loc. cit.*
87. *Loc. cit.*
88. *Shulchan Aruch—Orach Chayim*, 493:1.
89. Desser, *op. cit.*, p. 3.
90. *Loc. cit.*
91. *Loc. cit.*
92. Desser, *op. cit.*, p. 4.

93. *Loc. cit.*
94. Reference is to *Leviticus* XIX:18.
95. *Cf.* Gittin 55b-56a.
96. The Talmud relates that "Rabbi" was punished because he refused to have pity on a calf that ran towards him from the salughter, seeking protection. He turned the calf away saying, "For this [purpose] you were created." *Baba Metzia* 85a.
97. Desser, *op. cit.*, p. 4.
98. *Loc. cit.*
99. Desser, *op. cit.*, p. 4.
100. *Ibid.*, p. 6. Note that the same program of study was adopted as a basis for the Beth Yaacov schools for girls in Palestine. *Cf.* Dessler, *op. cit.*, Appendix, p. 1.
101. Abraham Zamba, "Mathivtha' BeVarshah," in Mirsky, *op. cit.*, pp. 365-380, pp. 368-369. Note that the spelling is *Mesivta* in Eisenstein, op. cit., p. 371.
102. *Ibid.*, p. 371.
103. Hilel Zaidman, "Yeshivoth Kether Torah MeYisudo shel HaRaoi MeRadomsk," in Mirsky, *op. cit.*, pp. 381-392.
104. *Ibid.*, p. 385.
105. *Ibid.*, p. 383-384.
106. *Loc. cit.*
107. Zamba, *op. cit.*, in Mirsky, *op. cit.*, pp. 355-361.
108. *Ibid.*, p. 355.
109. *Ibid.*, p. 386-357.
110. *Ibid.*, p. 356.
111. *Loc. cit.*
112. Elchanan Indelman, " 'Tarbuth' BePolin, Mekorah Vegidulah, Chazonah Ve-Chilyonah," *HaChinuch Vehatarbuth HaYivrith B'Eyropah bein Shete: Milchamoth Haolam*, Scharfstein, *op. cit.*, pp. 107-134.
113. *Ibid.*, p. 124-125.
114. *Ibid.*, p. 128-129.
115. Shevach Eden, "HaMachon LeMadaei HaYahadoth BeVarshah," in Mirsky, *op. cit.*, pp. 562-584 and 564-565.
116. *Ibid.*, p. 567.
117. *Ibid.*, p. 570.
118. Eden, *op. cit.*, in Mirsky, *op. cit.*, p. 569.
119. J. Michael, "Beth HaMidrash LeRabbanim BeVarshah," in Mirsky, *op. cit.*, pp. 585-603, and pp. 587, 590.
120. *Ibid.*, pp. 590, 598, 599.
121. *Ibid.*, p. 603.
122. *American Jewish Yearbook*, Vol. 60, 1959, p. 217.
123. *Ibid.*, Vol. 61, 1960, p. 266.
124. *Ibid.*, pp. 527-528. See Appendix p. 1 and statement concerning Posekim and the Shulchan Aruch.
125. *Ibid.*, p. 529.
126. Menachem M. Brayer, "HaChinuch HaYivri BeBesarabia," in Scharfstein, *op. cit.*, pp. 255-267, 257-258.
127. *Ibid.*, p. 262.

128. *American Jewish Yearbook*, Vol. 60, 1959, p. 220.
129. Zevi Yaacov Abraham, "Al HaYeshivoth BeHungaria HaNerchavah-Transylvania, Slovakia, Burgland, VeYugoslavia-1914-1944," in Mirsky, *op. cit.*, pp. 435-447.
130. *Ibid.*, p. 442. *Cf.* Aaron First, "Chisul Hachinuch Hayehudi BeHungaria," *Sheviley Hachinuch*, Vol. X, No. 2, pp. 55-63, March 1950.
131. Abraham, *op. cit*, p. 442.
132. *Loc. cit.*
133. *Loc. cit.*
134. *Ibid.*, pp. 442-443.
135. Abraham, *op. cit.*, p. 445.
136. Itzechak Isaac Halevi Jungreises, *"Yeshivoth Chatham Sofer BePressburg,"* in Mirsky, *op. cit.*, pp. 449-515.
137. *Ibid.*, p. 468. *Cf.* Yuda Leib Shill, *Sefer Minhagei Hachatham Sofer*, Erlav, 1950, p. 14.
138. *Ibid.*, p. 484.
139. Jungreiss, *op. cit.*, pp. 489-490.
140. *Ibid.*, pp. 501-502.
141. *Ibid.*, p. 515. *Cf.* Mark Vishnitzer, "Chomer LeToledoth HaYeshivoth BeEyropah HaMizrachith BeShnoth 1919-1939." *Talpioth*, Vol. V, Nos. 1-2, December 1950, pp. 157-175. On pp. 164-166, the author gives a complete list of the sixty-one yeshivoth which still existed in Hungary in 1939. These yeshivoth were of orthodox origin. It may be assumed that the study of the Shulchan Aruch was pursued in them.
142. *The American Jewish Yearbook*, Vol. 60, 1959, p. 226.
143. *Ibid.*, Vol. 61, 1960, p. 272.
144. Vishnitzer, *op. cit.*, pp. 157-175, 168-169. Vishnitzer notes that over thirty yeshivahs existed in Slovakia between the years 1919-1938 (pp. 166-167). The most important of these were the Yeshivah Chasam Sofer at Bratislava (*loc. cit.*); the Yeshivah Etz Chayim at Slatinske Doly (pp. 169-170).
145. *Ibid.*, pp. 157-175.
146. Mordechai Eilav, "HaChinuch HaYivri BeGermaniah BaTekufah Shebein Shetei Milchamoth HaOlam HaAcharonoth," *HaChinuch VeHaTarbuth HaYivrith BeEyropah Bein Shetei Milchamoth HaOlam*, 1957, pp. 1-42.
147. *Ibid.*, p. 9-13.
148. Eliahu Morpurgo in *Hameasef*, 1786, pp. 67-68.
149. Mordechai Eliav, *Hachinuch Hayehudi Bagermania Bimay HaHaskalah VeHaEmantzipatzia* (Jewish Education in Germany in the period of Enlightenment and Emancipation), Hotzoath Hasofarim shel Hasochnuth HaYehudith L'Eretz Israel, p. 53. *Cf.* pp. 54-57 for propositions of similar programs of study. The Italian name of "Morpurgo" seems to be derived from the city of Marburg, now Yugoslavia.
150. *Ibid.*, pp. 53-54. It is assumed that the reference is to the Shulchan Aruch. Note that the Shulchan Aruch was taught in Spanish and Italian Jewish schools.
151. Eliav, *op. cit.*, p. 313.
152. *Ibid.*, p. 157. In 1796, in Halberstadt, Germany, a modern Jewish orthodox religious school, Hasheorath Zevi, named after Zevi Hirsch Kaslin, was founded

with the purpose of educating the poor, helping them adjust to life in contemporary society. In 1805 a modern school, the Talmud Torah in Hamburg, was established by Rabbi Menachem Fankfurter, the grandfather of R.S.R. Hirsch, who served as rabbi of Altona. (pp. 159-161) *Cf.*, Bernard Drachman, "Samson Raphael Hirsch," p. xii in Samson Raphael Hirsch, *The Nineteen Letters of Ben Uziel*, translated from the German by Bernard Drachman.

153. Eliav, *op. cit.*, pp. 231 ff.
154. Eliav, *op. cit.*, pp. 231-232. It is of interest to note that until 1871 this school was co-educational in the lower classes. Thus in 1853 the first four grades were co-educational, and in 1857 only the first three grades were co-educational. In 1871 a separate girls' school was established.
155. *Ibid.*, pp. 234-235.
156. *Ibid.*, p. 236.
157. *Ibid.*, pp. 235-236.
158. *Ibid.*, pp. 236-237.
159. *Ibid.*, p. 237. Some other schools of this type are: Talmud Torah, Mosad LeHoroath Talmud, Mosad LeHoroath Torah.
160. Eliav, *op. cit.*, p. 237. Other religious schools that existed in different parts of Germany during the middle of the nineteenth century are mentioned on p. 338, and on pp. 149-153. Rabbi A. Hildescheimer has a detailed list of the existing Yeshivoth at the time in his work, *Uber die Jeschiba-Angelegenheit*, etc.
161. Mosheh Avigdor Shulvass, "Beth HaMedrash LeRabanim BeBerlin," *Mosedoth Torah B'Eyropeah Bevinianim UbeChurbanam*, in Mirsky, *op. cit.*, pp. 689-713.
162. *Ibid.*, pp. 698-699 and 708.
162. *Ibid.*, pp. 698-699 and 708.
163 Mordechai Eliav, "HaYeshivoth BeGermaniah," in Mirsky, *op. cit.*, pp. 419-424. From 1910 to the end of World War I, this was the only yeshivah in Germany. (*Loc. cit.*)
164. Yehudah Rosenthal, "Beth Hamedrash LeRabanim Berlin," in Mirsky, *op. cit.*, pp. 655-687, pp. 662 and 668. *Cf.*, Uri Kober, "Beth Hamedrash LeRabanim BeBreslau," *op. cit.*, pp. 605-633.
165. Eliav, *op. cit.*, p. 326.
166. M. Lazarus, *Trau und Frei*, pp. 69ff. Quoted in Eliav, *op. cit.*, pp. 326-327.
167. Rosenthal, *op. cit.*, in Mirsky, *op. cit.*, pp. 655-687, pp. 662 and 668. *Cf.* Kober, *op. cit.*, pp. 605-633.
168. Eliav, *op. cit.*, p. 422.
169. Sections 69-78 deal with the salting of meat in preparation for cooking.
170. Sections 91-97 deal with the handling of dairy and meat products. Sections 98-104 deal with mixed foods, permitted and forbidden.
171. Eliav, *op. cit.*, p. 423.
172. these sections deal with various laws pertaining to the Sabbath.
173. These sections deal with the laws pertaining to various holidays.
174. These sections deal with forbidden foods.
175. Rosenthal, *op. cit.*, pp. 662 and 668.
176. Eliav, *op. cit.*, pp. 16-21. *Cf. ibid.*, pp. 26-32 for cities where such high schools were established.

177. *Ibid.*, pp. 35-41. Two articles dealing with Jewish education in Germany deserve mention here: Eliezer L. Ehrman, "Jewish Education in Germany,'*Jewish Education*, Vol. XI, September 1939, pp. 91-100; and Joshua Trachtenberg, "Jewish Education in Eastern Europe at the Beginning of the Seventeenth Century," *Jewish Education, op. cit.*, pp. 121-137.
178. H. Lewis, "Jewish Education in London," *Jewish Education*, Vol. X, No. 2, April-June 1938, pp. 70-76. The three types of Jewish schools were adminstered by the Talmud Torah Trust, the Jewish Religion Education Board, and the Union of Religion Classes, p. 71. *Cf.* Appendix, p. 10.
179. *Ibid.*, p. 72.
180. *Jews' College, London Hundred and Third Annual Report*, March 24, 1980, p. 60. *Cf.* Theodore H. Caster, "England," *Universal Jewish Encyclopedia*, Vol. IV, pp. 110-130.
181. *Ibid.*, p. 44.
182. *Ibid.*, p. 47.
183. *Jews' College . . . Report, op. cit.*, pp. 49-50, 54-55.
184. *Ibid.*, pp. 68-69.
185. *Ibid.*, p. 78, section (d) and p. 80. See also the syllabus for examination, pp. 87 and 91.
186. *The American Jewish Yearbook*, vol. 58, 1957, p. 242. *Cf.* Gaster, *op. cit.*, pp. 110-130.
187. Gaster, *op. cit.*
188. *Ibid.*, p. 130.
189. *Loc. cit.*
190. *Cf.* Letter from Dr. H.Z. Sipper, Education Director of the Association for Promoting Torah Education in London, dated July 21, 1961. Appendix, p. 11, and 37-37b and 38-38a.
191. The course is conducted by Mr. Carmell, Chairman of the Association. See letter referred to in the preceding note.
192. M. Avigail, "Tochnith Halimudim Beveith HaSefer HaYesodi BeYisrael," in *Fundamental Principles for Diaspora Education*, Proceedings of Institute on Diaspora Education held under the auspices of the Jewish Agency at Zofith Israel, on August 14,18, 1955, pp. 48-52. *Cf.* pp. 59-63.
193. *Misrad HaChinuch YahaTarbuth, Tochnith HaLimudin LeVeith HaSefer HaYesodi HaMamlachti HaDathi*, Grade Four; *cf.* the article by J. Geldschmidt, "Religious Education in Israel," *Jewish Education*, Spring 1958, dedicated to Israel's tenth anniversary, pp. 29-34 and 57, where life at a yeshivah is described and the syllabus of the religious state schools is discussed (pp. 31, 33).
194. Misrad Hachinuch, *op. cit.*, p. 19. A brochure, *Halichoth Olam*, is used for grades 5-8.
195. *Chovreth HaPesach* by I. Berman. Eliezer Rieger in *Hachinuch Yayivra B'Eretz Israel, Hamatarah VaHatochnith*, pp. 114, 246 and 247, lists schools that offer religious education. On p. 252 he notes that the Hertzliah Gymnasium and the Beth Hasefer HaReali, both boys' schools in Tel Aviv and Haifa respectively, each offer courses in Halachah and Agadah. *Cf.* also letter from the Israeli Office of Education and Culture, dated March 12, 1961, in Appendix.

196. Shelomo Simon Grimberg, "Chinuch Dathi," *Encyclopedia Chinuchith*, Misrad HaChinuch VenTarbuth UMosad Bialik publishers, pp. 362-377. See p. 371. We note that in some schools the Bible and the Talmud are studied as part of the humanities, *Cf.* M. Avigail, "Tochnith Halimudim LeKitoth Beit-Gimmel," (The Program of Study in Grades B and C), *Madrich LeKitoth Beth-Gimmel*. HaVaad HaPoel—Merkaz in LeTarbuth UlChinuch, HaHistadruth Haklalith shel Ha-Ovedim HaYivrim B'Eretz Israel, pp. 82-83 and 103. *Cf.*, Yosef Bentwitz, *HaChinuch BiMdinath Israel*, p. 36, referring to the Chibbath Zion schools. Note also the letter from Mr. I. L. Benor of the Ministry of Education in Israel, indicating that the Shulchan Aruch proper or in an abbreviated form, is officially studied in Israel. *Cf.*, Appendix, p. 13.
197. The *Mishnah Berurah* is the name given to the Shulchan Aruch edited by Rabbi Isroel Meir HaCohen; it contains the latest decisions followed by almost all Ashkenazic Jews.
198. See letter from E. Rothschild of the Neveh Shalom office of the Ozar Hatorah organization in Casablanca, dated August 24, 1961, Appendix, p. 15.
199. Levy M. Becker and Louis Rosenberg, "Jewish Education in Montreal," *Jewish Education*, Vol. XXII, No. 1-2, Winter-Spring, pp. 63-71, p. 63.
200. this information is derived from a communication received by this writer from Mr. Samuel Lewin, Educational Representative of the Canadian Jewish Congress in Montreal. The letter is dated June 20, 1961. We note that in Canada, the Shulchan Aruch is in the process of being translated into English, pointing to the importance of the Code there. *Cf.* Appendix, p. 16.
201. Becker and Rosenberg, *op. cit.*, p. 63.
202. Becker and Rosenberg, *op. cit.*, p. 64.
203. *Ibid.*, p. 65. *Cf.* American Jewish Yearbook, Vol. 61, 1960, pp. 178179, and *ibid.*, Vol. 59, 1958, pp. 234-235.

BIBLIOGRAPHY

I. Primary Sources

Asaf, Simcha, *Mekoroth Letoledoth Hachinuch Be Israel* (Sources of the History of Jewish Education), Tel Aviv: "Dvir" Publishing Company, Vol. I, 1954 (second printing); Vol. II, 1931; Vol. III, 1973; Vol. 14, 1947.

Caro, Joseph, *Beth Yosef—Commentary on Arba Turim* by R. Yaacov ben Asher. Jerusalem: "El Hamekoroth" Publishing Company Ltd., 1958.

Caro, Joseph, *Introduction—Shulchan Aruch Choshen Mishpat* (Part I). New York: I.Z. Pollack, 1943.

Caro, Joseph, *Introduction, Tur Orach Chayim*, by Yacov ben Asher. Warsaw: Argelbrand Brothers Publishers, 1882.

Caro, Joseph, *Introduction, Yad Hachazakah* by Moses ben Maimon. New York: Ramba'M Publishing Company, 1956.

Caro, Joseph, *Shulchan Aruch*; Part I, *Orach Chayim*; Part II, *Yoreh Deah*; Part III, *Even Haezer*; Part IV, *Chosen Mishpat*. Lemberg: Druck und Verlag des J. Madfes, 1876.

Epstein, Isidore (editor) *The Talmud* (sub-title: *The Babylonian Talmud*). London: The Soncino Press:

Seder Zera'Im, Vol. I (*Berakoth* 14a, 28a, 30b), translated by Maurice Simon, 1958.

Seder Moed, Vols. I and II (*Shabbath* I, 17a and b, 18b, 19a, 109a, 119a and b, 151b), translated by Rabbi Dr. H. Freedman, 1938.

Seder Moed, Vol. IV. (*Pesachim*, 116b) translated by Rabbi Dr. H. Freedman, 1938.

Seder Moed, Vol. V (*Yoma* 18a, 83a, 84b) translated by Rabbi Dr. Leo Jung, 1938.

Seder Moed, Vol. VI (*Sukkah*, 28a) translated into English by Rabbi Dr. Israel W. Slotki, 1938.

Seder Moed, Vol. VII (*Taanith*, 11a, 25a) translated by Maurice Simon, 1938.

Seder Nezikin, Vol. I (*Baba Kama*, 113a and b) translated by E. W. Kirzner, 1935.

Güdemann, M., *Quellenschriften zur Geschichte des Unterrichts und der Erziehung bei den deutschen Juden—von den altesten Zeiten bis auf Mendelsohn*. Berlin: A. Hofmann und Comp., 1891.

Seder Nezikin, Vol. 11 (*Baba Metzia*, 84b) translated by Rabbi Dr. H. Freedman, 1935.

Seder Nezikin, Vol. III (*Baba Bathra* I, 8a, 9a, 10a, 21a) translated by Maurice Simon, 1935.

Seder Nezikin, Vol. VIII (*Aboth* II, 5; III, 2, 3, and 18; V, 21) translated by J. Israelstam, London, 1935.

Seder Nashim, Vol. II (*Yebamoth* II, 109b) translated by Israel W. Slotki (Rev. Dr.), 1936.

Seder Nashim, Vols. III and IV (*Kethuboth* 50a, 67b, 105a) translated by Israel W. Slotki (Rev. Dr.), 1936.

Seder Nashim, Vol. VI (*Nedarim* 41a, 81a) translated by Rabbi Dr. H. Freedman, 1936.

Seder Nashim, Vol. VI (*Sotah* 47b) translated by Rabbi B. D. Klein, 1936.

Seder Nashim, Vol. VIII, (*Kiddushin*, 29b, 30a, 33b) translated by H. Freedman (Rabbi Dr.), 1936.

Leteris, Meir Halevi (Editor), *The Bible* (Old Testament). New York: Hebrew Publishing company (no date given):

Genesis XXXIX, 10.

Exodus XII, 4-9; XVIII, 21-22; XX, 12; XXI, 19; XXIII, 8, 12; XXVIII, 15, 17, 30.

Leviticus XI, 43; XIV, 4; XIX, 10, 14, 16, 18, 35; XXI, 3, 19; XXIII, 22; XXXIII, 40.

Numbers XI, 29; XV, 16, 29, 38-39; XVIII, 17.

Deuteronomy IV, 9, 24; V, 14, 16; VI, 8-9; X, 19; XI, 19; XX, 7-8; XVI, 19-20; XIX, 19; XXII, 1, 4; XXIII, 11-15; XXIV, 10-13; XXV, 13-16; XXX, 4.

Joshua I:8.

I Samuel, V, 8; VI, 12.

II Kings XXV, 22.

Isaiah II, 22; III, 9; XXVIII, 9; XXXVIII, 19; LII, 21; LVII, 7.

Jeremiah XXIX, 7.

Zechariah VIII, 16.

Psalms I, 1; V, 8.

Proverbs III, 6; IV, 13; X, 12; XXII, 6; XXIV, 11; XXVI, 6.

Ecclesiastes, XI, 1.

Maimonides (Rabbi Moses ben Maimon), *Yad Hackazakah*, also known as *Mishneh Torah*. New York: Ramba'M Publishing Company, 1956.

Pollack, Mosheh Chayim (Editor) *Mishnah, The*. New York: Orah Publishing Company, 1946.

Yaacov (R.) ben Asher, *Arba Turim*, (Vol. I, *Tur Orach Chayim*; Vol. II, *Tur Yoreh Deah*; Vol. III, *Tur Even Haezer*; Vol. IV, *Tur Choshen Mishpat*). Warsaw: Argelbrand Brothers, Publishers, 1882.

II. Secondary Sources

A. LITERATURE ON JOSEPH CARO AND THE SHULCHAN ARUCH

Abraham, Ben Eliahu, *Introduction—Shulchan Aruch Orah Chayim*, New York: Mefitzey Torah Publishing Company, 1951.

Ashkenazi, David, *Sefer Kore Hadoroth*. Pietrkov: Aaron Walden, Publisher, 1895.

Avida, Yehudah, "Rishonay Mishpachath Caro B'Eretz Israel" ("The First Settlers of the Caro Family in Israel"), *Jerusalem Research on Israel*, Yish Shalom, Michael Yish Shalom, editor. Jerusalem: Mosad Harav Cook Publishing Company, 1953.

Azulai, Chayim David (Chid'O), *Maarecheth Gedolim—Maarecheth Sefarim*, Itzchak ben Yaacov, editor. Jerusalem: "Sefer" Publishing Company, 1954. First printing Vilna, 1863.

ben Eliahu, Abraham, *Introduction—Shulchan Aruch Orach Chayim*. New York: Mefitzay Torah Publishing company, 1951.

Bloch, Joseph S., "The Shulchan Aruch—Its Origin, Validity, and Significance," *Israel and the Nations*. Berlin: Benjamin Hartz, 1927. Chapter V, pp. 53-91.

De Sola Pool, David, "The Traditional Code of Jewish Education," *Menorah Journal*, X, (June-July, 1924), pp. 267-281.

Ginzberg, Asher (Rav Tzair), "Hashulchan Aruch," *Hashiloah*, I-IV, (July-December, 1898).

Ginzberg, Louis, "Caro, Joseph B. Ephraim," *The Jewish Encyclopedia*, Isidore Singer, editor. New York: Funk and Wagnalls Company, 1903, Vol. III, pp. 583-589.

Gordon, Hirsch Loeb, *The Maggid of Caro*. New York: The Shoulson Press, 1949.

Greenwald, Leopold, *Harav R. Joseph Caro Uzmano* ("Rabbi Joseph Caro and his Time"). New York; Philip Feldhiem, 1954.

Halpern, Israel, *Pinkas Vaad Arba Aratzoth* ("Minutes of the Council of Four Lands"). Jerusalem: Mosad Bialik, 1945.

Hones, Shimon Mosheh, *Sefer Toledoth Haposekim*. New York: "Halachah" Publishing Company, 1946.

Isserles, Moses, *Introduction, Shulchan Aruch Choshen Mishpat*, Part II. New York: Mop Press Inc., 1953.

Jung, Rabbi Leo, *Essentials of Judaism*. New York: Union of Orthodox Jewish Congregations of America, 1953. (Tenth edition).

Kagan, Rabbi Israel Meir Hacohen, *Introduction, Mishnah Berurah*. New York: Shulsinger Brothers Publishing Company, 1952.

Margoliouth, Reuven, "Defusay HaShulchan Aruch Harishonim," *Sinai*, XXXVII (Nisan-Elul, 1956), Jerusalem.

Margolis, Ephrayim, *Introduction—Shulchan Aruch Orach Chayim*. New York: Mefitzay Torah Publishing Company, 1951.

R. Chayim of Volozin, *Introduction—Shulchan Aruch Orach Chayim*. New York: Mefitzay Torah Publishing Company, 1951.

Ravkesh, Rabbi Mosheh, *Introduction—Shulchan Aruch Orach Chayim*. New York: Mefitzay Torah Publishing Company, 1951.

Spector, Itzchak, *The Ethics of the Shulchan 'Aruk*. Tacoma, Washington: Uraitha Publishing Company, 1930.

Spector, Itzchak, "The Origin and Development of the Shulchan 'Aruk," *The Reflex*, IV, (May 1929), Chicago, Illinois, pp. 22-26.

Weiss, Isaac Hirsch, *Dor Dor Vedorshov*. Vilna: 1911, Part V, Sixth Edition.

B. HISTORY AND PRINCIPLES OF EDUCATION, JEWISH AND NON-JEWISH

Anderson, Vernon E., Grimm, Paul R., and Gruhn, William T., *Principles and Practices of Secondary Education*. New York: The Ronald Press, 1951.

Berman, Jeremiah J., "Jewish Education in New York City, 1860-1900," *Yivo Annual of Jewish Social Studies*, IX. New York: Yiddish Scientific Institute, 1954. Pp. 247-275.

Bienenstock, Theodore, "Democratic Leadership and Fellowship in the School Program," *Journal of Educational Sociology*, XXVII, (May, 1954).

Brubacher, John S., *Modern Philosophies of Education* (Second edition, second impression). New York: McGraw-Hill Book company, Inc., 1950.

Butler, Donald, *Four Philosophies and their Practice in Education and Religion*. New York: Harper and Brothers, 1957 (revised edition).

Chipkin, Israel S., "Jewish Education in the United States at the Mid-Century," *The Jewish Education Register and Directory*, 1951.

Chipkin, Israel S., "Twenty-Five Years of Jewish Education in the United States," *The American Jewish Yearbook*, XXXVIII, September 17, 1936 to September 5, 1937. Philadelphia: The American Jewish Committee, The Jewish Publication Society of America.

Church, Joseph, *Childhood and Adolescence*. New York: Random House, 1957.

Corey, Arthur F., "Leadership in a Corporate Society," *Phi Delta Kappah* XXXV, (April, 1954).

Cox, Philip W. L., and Long, Forrest E., *Principles of Secondary Education*. New York: D. C. Heath, 1932.

Curoe, Philip R. V., *Principles of Education*. New York: Globe Book Company, 1926.

"Curriculum Development in the Elementary Schools," *Curiculum Bulletin No. 1.*, 1955-1956.

Dewey, John, *Democracy and Education*. New York: The Macmillan Company, 1920.

Dewey, John, *The School and Society* (second edition). Chicago: University of Chicago Press, 1915.

Drazin, Nathan, *History of Jewish Education from 515 B.C.E. to 220 C.E.* Baltimore-The Johns Hopkins Press, 1940.

Dushkin, Alexander M., *Jewish Education in New York City* (to 1918). New York: The Bureau of Jewish Education, 1918.

Dushkin, Alexander M., and Engelman, Uriah Zevi, *Jewish Education in the United States*, Report of the Commission for the Study of Jewish Education in the United States. New York: American Association for Jewish Education, 1959. Vol. I.

Eels, William H., "Motivating Students for Civic Responsibilities," *Current Issues in Higher Education*, Proceedings (March 1953), pp. 106-109.

Elfenbein, Israel, "Jewish Education in Palestine under Turkey; 1519-1919," *B'rocho L'Mnachem*. Norman Paris (editor). (Festive edition) St. Louis: The United Orthodox Jewish Community, 1955, pp. 53-70.

Eliav, Mordecai, *Hachinuch Hayehudi BeGermania Bimay HaHaskalah Vehaemantzipatziah* ("Jewish Education in Germany during the Haskalah and the Emancipation Movements"). Jerusalem: Hotzoath Hosefarim Shel Hasochenuth Hayehudith L'Eretz Israel, 1961.

Eliav, Mordecai and Kleinberg, F.A., *Mekoroth Letholedoth Hachinuch BeIsrael Uveamim* ("Sources of Education in Israel and the Nations"). Tel Aviv: "Otzar Hamoreh" Hotzoath Hasefarim Shel Histadruth Hamorim, publishers, Yalkut Gimmel, 1960.

Engelman, Uriah Zevi, "Trends and Developments in Jewish Education, 1945-1946," *The American-Jewish Yearbook* (1945-1946).

Engelman, Uriah Zevi, "The Congregation and Hebrew Education," *Jewish Education*, XXIV, (Fall, 1953).

Fishman, Isidore, *The History of Jewish Education in Central Europe from the End of the Sixteenth Century to the Eighteenth Century*. London: Edward L. Goldston, 1944.

Fox, Mildred G., "Providing for the Gifted," *Education Digest*, XIX (February, 1954).

Gates, Arthur I., *Teaching Reading*. Washington, D.C.: Department of Classroom Teachers: American Educational Research Association of the National Education Association, June 1953.

Glueck, Sheldon, "The Home, the School and Delinquency," *The Harvard Educational Review*, XIII, (January-December, 1953), pp. 17-33.

Grace, Alonzo G., "Educational Progress," *Phi Delta Kappah*, XXXIII, (November, 1951), pp. 122-126.

Graves, Frank Pierrepont, *A History of Education* (During the Middle Ages and the Transition to Modern Times). New York: The Macmillan Company, 1912.

Greenstone, Julius H., "Jewish Education in the United States," *American-Jewish Yearbook*. Philadelphia: The Jewish Publication Society of America, September 1914.

Grinstein, Hyman B., *The Rise of the Jewish Community of New York, 1654-1680*. Philadelphia: The Jewish Publication Society of America, 1954.

Guenther, H.W., "Character Education is Everybody's Business," *Phi Delta Kappah* XXIV, (May, 1953).

Gwynn, John M., *curriculum Principles and Social Trends*. New York: Macmillan Company, 1950.

Handschin, Charles H., *Modern Language Teaching*. New York: World Book Company, 1940.

Havighurst, Robert J., and Neugarten, Bernice L., *Society and Education*. Boston; Allyn and Bacon, Inc. 1957.

Honor, Leo L., "The Impact of the American Environment and the American Ideas on Jewish Education," *The Jewish Quarterly Review*, XIV, (April, 1955), pp. 451-496.

Horne, Herman Harrel, *The Psychological Principles of Education*, London: Macmillan and Company, Ltd., 1916.

Jones, Vernon, "Character Education," *Encyclopedia of Educational Research*, third edition. New York: The Macmillan Company, 1960, pp. 184-190.

Kilpatrick, William H., *Education for a Changing Civilization*. New York: The Macmillan Company, 1932.

Klapper, Paul, *Principles of Educational Practice*. New York: D. Appleton and Company, 1912.

Kober, Adolph, "Emancipation's Impact on the Education and Vocational Training of German Jewry," *Jewish Social Studies*, XVI, New York, (January and April, 1954), No. 1, pp. 3-33; No. 2, pp. 151-176.

Korn, Bertram W., "Eventful Years and Experiences: Studies in the Nineteenth Century American Jewish History," *American Jewish Archives*. Cincinnati: 1954.

Lull, Herbert G., *Principles of Elementary Education*. New York: W.W. Norton and Company, Inc., 1935.

Mayer Frederick, "Education and Religion," *Phi Delta Kappah*, XXXVI, (June, 1955), pp. 245-248.

McGhee, Paul A., "Higher Education and Adult Education: Four Questions," *Current Issues in Higher Education, 1953 Proceedings of the Eighth conference on Higher Education*, Chicago, Illinois, March 5-7, 1953. (Frances H. Horn, Editor).

Melby, Ernest O., "Leadership in an Age of Anxiety," *Phi Delta Kappah*, XIV, (June, 1953).

Melby, Ernest O., "The Forward Look," *Journal of Educational Sociology, The*, XXIV, (February, 1951).

Meyer, Adolph E., *The Development of Education in the 20th Century*. New York: Prentice Hall, 1949.

Miller, Bernette, *The Palace School of Mohammad the Conqueror*. Cambridge: Harvard University Press, 1941.

Moore, Willis, "Indoctrination versus Education," *The American Association of University Professors*, XXXVIII, (Summer, 1953), pp. 220-229.

Payne, George Enoch, *Principles of Educational Sociology*. New York: New York University Press, 1928.

Pilch, Judah, "Jewish Religious Education," *Religious Education, a Comprehensive Survey*. New York: Abingdon Press, 1960, pp. 382-395. Marvin J. Taylor (editor).

Risk, Thomas M., *Principles and Practices of Teaching in Secondary Schools*, second edition. New York: American Book Company, 1947.

Rudavsky, David, "Nature and Extent of Secondary Schooling in America," *Jewish Education*, XII, (April, 1940).

Rudavsky, David, "Trends in Jewish School Organization and Enrollment in New York City, 1917-1950," *Yivo Annual of Jewish Social Science*, Vol. X. New York: Yivo Institute for Jewish Research, 1955.

Sassani, Abdul H.K., *Education in Turkey*. Washington, D.C.: U.S. Government Printing Office, U.S. Office of Education, *Bulletin No. 10*, 1952.

Scharfstein, Zevi, *Toledoth Hachinuch BeIsrael Bedoroth Haacharonim* ("History of Jewish Education in Modern Times"). New York: Ogen Publishing Company, Vol. I, 1945; Vol. II, 1947.

Schorling, Raleigh, *Student Teaching*, second edition, fourth impression. New York: McGraw-Hill Book Company, Inc., 1949.

Sherrill, Lewis Joseph, *The Rise of Christian Education*. New York: The MacMillan Company, 1944.

Silver, Louis, "The Jews in Albany, New York, 1860-1900," *Yivo Annual of Jewish Social Science*, IX, New York: 1954, pp. 212-246.

Smiley, Marjorie B., *Intergroup Education and the American College*. New York: Teachers College, Columbia University, 1952.

Society for Curriculum Study (The), *An Evaluation of Modern Education*. New York: D. Appleton Century Company, 1942. J. Paul Leonard and Alvin P. Eurich, editors.

Stone, Larence Joseph, and Church, Joseph, *Childhood and Adolescence*. New York: Random House, 1957.

Strang, Ruth, *An Introduction to Child Study*. New York: The Macmillan Company, 1959, (fourth edition).

Swift, Fletcher H., *Education in Ancient Israel*. Chicago: The Open Court Publishing Company, 1919.

Symonds, Percyval M., *The Dynamics of Parent-Child Relationships*. New York: Bureau of Publications, Teachers College, Columbia University, 1949.

Taba, Hilda; Brady, Elizabeth Hall; Robinson, John T., *Intergroup Education in Public Schools*. Washington, D.C.: American Council on Education, 1952.

Thorndike, E. L., *Human Nature and the Social Order*. New York; The Macmillan Company, 1942.

Tibawi, Abdul Latif, *Arab Education in Mandatory Palestine*. London: Luzac Publishing Company, 1956.

Turner, C.E., *Principles of Health Education*. New York: D. C. Heath and Company, 1939.

Wheeler, Raymond Holder, *Principles of Mental Development*. New York: The Thomas Y. Crowell Company, 1932.

Whitehead, Alfred North, *The Aims of Education*. New York: The New American Library, 1951.

C. CURRICULA AND PERTINENT PUBLICATIONS

Associated Talmud Torahs of Chicago, *Tochnith HaLimudim Lechamesh Shenoth Limud BaTalmud Torah* ("A Talmud Torah Curriculum"). Chicago: January, 1960.

Avigail, M. "Tochnith Halimudim Beveit Hasefer Hayesodi BeYisrael," *Fundamental Princples for Diaspora Education, Proceedings* of Institute on Diaspora Education. Held under the auspices of the Jewish Agency at Zofith, Israel, on August 14-18, 1955.

Avigail, M., "Tochnith Halimudim Lekitoth Beit-Gimmel," ("The Program of Study for Grades B and C"), *Madrich Lekitoth Beth-Gimmel*. Tel Aviv: Havaad Hapoel-Merkaz LeTarbuth Ulechinuch, HaHistadruth Hakelalith Shel Haovdim Hayivrim B'Eretz Israel, 1958.

Board of Education of the City of New York, *Curriculum Development in the Elementary Schools*. New York: Curriculum Bulletin No. 1, 1955-56 Series, 1955. William Jansen, Superintendent of Schools.

Bortniker, Elijah, in cooperation with The Principals' Council Board of Education, Metropolitan Council, United Synagogue, *Outline of Studies for the First Year of the Congregational Hebrew School*. New York: Jewish Education Committee of New York, 1957. Dedicated to the memory of Leon Kohn.

Bortniker, Elijah, *Outline of Studies for the Second Year of the Congregational School*. New York: Jewish Education Committee of New York, 1960. Dedicated to the memory of Lillie Rubee.

Commission on Jewish Education of the Union of American Hebrew Congregatons and the Central Conference of American Rabbis, *An Outline of the Curriculum of the Jewish Religious School*. New York: The Union of American Hebrew Congregations, Eugene B. Borowitz, editor. Dedicated to Dr. Emanuel Gamorah. 1959-60.

Desler, N. Z., *Tochnith Halimudim, 1959 Beith Chinuch Hayivri*. Cleveland: Torah Umesorah, publishers, 1959.

Dushkin, Alexander M., and Engelman, Uriah Z., *Report of Commission for the Study of Jewish Education in the United States*. New York: American Association for Jewish Education, 1959.

Fendel, Zachary, *Yeshivah Preparatory High School, Forest Hills, L.I. Bulletin of General Information*. New York: 1959.

Frishberg, I.Z., *Tochnith Limudim Kelalith Lemosedoth Hachinuch Haamameim*. New York: Mizrachi National Education Committee, 1946.

Gemorah, Emanual, (editor), *A Curriculum for the Jewish Religious Schools*. Cincinnati: Union of American Hebrew Congregations, 1946-1947.

Hebrew Culture Service Committee, *Hebrew in Colleges and Universities*. New York: Hebrew Culture Service Committee for American High Schools and Colleges, 1958. Judah Lapson, editor.

Hebrew Union College—Jewish Institute of Religion, *Catalogue*, 1958-1959-1960.
Hurley, Beatrice David, *Curriculum for Elementary School Children*. New York: The Ronald Press Company, 1957.
Jewish Theological Seminary of America, *Register*. New York: 1959.
Jews' College-London, *Hundred and Third Annual Report*. London: 1960.
Machleket Hachinuch Shel HaSochnuth HaYehudith L'Eretz Israel, *Tochnith Halimudim Hanehugah Bevatey Safer Shel Hamizrachi*, IX. Jerusalem, 1932.
"Merkos L'Inyonei Chinuch," *Tochnith Limudim A. Lemosedoth Chinuch Lenarim B. Levotei Sefer Lanaaroth* ("A Program of Study for Boys' Schools and for Girls' Schools). New York: Merkos L'Inyonei Chinuch, Inc., publishers, 1944.
Misrad Hachinuch Vehatarbuth, *Tochnith Halimudim Leveith Hasefer Hayesodi Hamamlachti Hadathi, Grade Four*. Jerusalem: Government Printing Press, Tishri, 1957.
New York University, *School of Education Bulletin*, LXI, (May 15, 1961). New York: New York University, 1961-1962.
New York University Bulletin, *School of Education Announcement*, New York: New York University, 1961-1962.
Principals Council, The Associated United Synagogue Schools in Queens, *Course of Studies for Second Year*. New York: The Jewish Education Committee of New York, Inc., 1951.
Principals Council, The Associated United Synagogue Schools in Queens, *Course of Studies for Third Year*. New York: The Jewish Education Committee of New York, Inc., 1951.
Principals Council, The Associated United Synagogue Schools in Queens, *Course of Studies for Fourth Year*. New York: The Jewish Education Committee of New York, Inc., 1951.
Ruffman, Louis L., in cooperation with The Committee on Objectives, Standards and Curricula of the United Synagogue Commission on Jewish Education, and with the assistance of Abraham Segal, *Curriculum Outline for the Congregational School* (revised edition). New York: United Synagogue Commission on Jewish Education, 1959.
Union of American Hebrew Congregations, *A Curriculum for the Jewish Religious School*. Cincinnati: 1946-1947.
Vaad Hatochnith Shel Agudath Hamnahalim Hayivrim, *Tochnith LiMudim Levotei HaTalmud Torah* (Second Edition, Part I). New York: Jewish Publication Committee of New York, Inc., Menachem M. Edelstein, editor, 1950.
Yeshivah University Bulletin, *Stern College for Women, Catalogue 1959-61*. New York: 1959.
Yeshivah University, *Bulletin of General Information*, VII, (September, 1959).
The Hebrew High School of Greater New York, Marshalliah, *Jews in America*. New York: 1960.

III Other Writings
A. JEWISH, RELATED HISTORY, AND KINDRED WORKS
Abraham, Zevi Yaacov, "Al Hayeshivoth BeHungariah Hagedolah—Transylvania, Slovakia, Burgland, VeYugoslavia—1914-1944," *Mosedoth Torah B'Eyropah*

Bevinyanam Ubechurbanam. New York: Ogen Publishing House of Histadruth Ivrith of America, 1956, pp. 435-447.

Abrahams, Israel, *Jewish Life in the Middle Ages*. New York: The Macmillan Company, 1917.

Alcalay, Itzchak Abraham, "Hachinuch Hayivri BeYugoslavia, 1919-1941," *Hachinuch Vehatarbuth Hayivrith B'Eyropah*, Zevi Scharfstein, Editor. New York: Ogen Publishing House of Histadruth Ivrith of America, 1957.

Alfasi, Isaac, *Hilchoth Rav Alfas*. Vilna: Widow and Brothers RoM, Publishers, 1881.

Andrews, Fannie Fern, *the Holy Land under Mandate*. New York Houghton Mifflin Company, 1931.

Ashkenazi, Mordecai ben Hillel, *Sefer Hamordecai*, appended to the Talmud Bavli. New York: M'Oroth Publishing Company, 1960.

Bamberger, Bernard J., "The Reform View," *Judaism*. New York, National Committee of Contemporary Jewish Affairs, National Council of Jewish Women, 1944.

Bentwich, Norman, *Palestine*. London: Ernest Benn Ltd., 1934.

Bentwitz, Yosef, *Hachinuch BeMedinath Israel*. Tel-Aviv; Joshua Chachik, Publishing House, Ltd. 1916.

Bortniker, Elijah, "Jewish Education in Europe," *Jewish Education*, XXIX, (1959).

Bortniker, Elijah, "Report on Jewish Education in Europe," *Jewish Education*, XXIX, (Spring, 1953).

Brayer, Menachem M., "Hayeshivoth BeRomaniah," *Mosedoth Torah B'Eyropah BeVinyanam Ubechurbanam*. New York: Ogen Publishing House of Histadruth Ivrith of America, 1957. Zevi Sharfstein, Editor.

Brayer, Menachem M., "Hachinuch Hayivri BeTransylvania," *Hachinuch Vehatarbuth Hayivrith B'Eyropah*. New York: Ogen Publishing House of Histadruth Ivrith of America, 1957. Zevi Scharfstein, Editor.

Bregstone, Philip P., *Chicago and Its Jews—A Cultural History*. Privately published, 1933. (Place not indicated.)

Brickman, William W., "A Visit to Soviet Jewry," *Orthodox Jewish Life*. New York: Union of Orthodox Jewish Congregations of America, XXV, (February, 1958).

Brickner, Barnett R., "The History of Jewish Education in Cincinnati," *Jewish Education*, VIII, (October-December, 1936).

Caro, Joseph, *Kesef Mishneh, on Yad Hachazakah by Maimonides*. New York: RAMBA'M Publishing Company, 1956.

Caro, Joseph, *Maggid Maysharim*, Jerusalem: "Orah" Publishing Company, 1960.

Caro, Joseph, *Sh'eloth U'Teshuvoth Beth Yosef*. Jerusalem: Tifereth Hatorah Publishing Company, 1960. Bezalel Landau, Editor. (Old edition: Salonica: Mosheh di Medina and Shemuel Kaleb, publishers, 1599.)

Castro, Americo, *Espana en su Historia—Christianos Moros y Judios*, ("Spain in its History of Christians, Moors, and Jews"). Buenos Aires: Editorial Losada, S.A., 1948.

Cohen, Morris Raphael, *A Dreamer's Journey* (autobiography). Glencoe, Illinois: The Free Press, 1949.

Cohon, Beryl D., *Judaism in Theory and Practice*. New York: Bloch Publishing Company, 1948.

Cordovero, Moses, *Tomer Devorah*. New York: Shoshanim Publishing Company, 1960.

Creasy, Sir Edward S., *History of the Ottoman Turks*, second edition. London: Richard Bentley and Son, 1877.

DiJour, Ilya., "Latin America," *The American-Jewish Yearbook*, LXI. New York: The American Jewish Committee, 1960.

DiJour, Ilya, "Latin America," *The American Jewish Yearbook,* LXII. New York: The American Jewish Committee, 1961.

Dubnow, Simon Markovich, *History of the Jews in Russia and Poland*. Translated from the Russian by I. Friedlander. Philadelphia: The Jewish Publication Society, 1916.

Eden, Shevach, "HaMachon Lemadrey Hayahaduth BeVarshab," *Mosedoth Torah B'Eyropah Bevinyanam Ubechurbanam*. New York: Ogen Publishing House of Histadruth Ivrith of America, 1956.

Eisenstein, Miriam, *Jewish Schools in Poland*, 1919-1939. New York: King's Crown Press, 1950.

Elbogen, Ismar, *A Century of Jewish Life*. Philadelphia: The Jewish Publication Society of America, 1953. Translated from the German by Moses Hadas.

Eliash, Mordecai, "Hayeshivoth BeGermania," *Mosedoth Torah B'Eyropah Bevinyanam Ubechurbanam*. New York: Ogen Publishing House of Histadruth Ivrith of America, 1956.

Engelman, Uriah Zevi, "Jewish Education and Social Research," *Jewish Social Service Quarterly*, XXVIII, (June, 1952).

Esco Foundation for Palestine, Inc., *Palestine, A Study of Jewish, Arab, and British Policies*. New Haven: Yale University Press, 1947.

First, Aaron, "Chissul Hachinuch Hayehudi BeHungaria," *Sheviley Hachinuch*, X (March, 1950), pp. 55-63.

Fuss, I., "Hachinuch Hayivri BeBelgia Beyn Shetey Milchamoth Haolam," *Hachinuch Vehatharbuth Hayivrith B'Eyropah*. New York: Ogen Publishing House of Histadruth Ivrith of America, 1957. Zevi Scharfstein, Editor.

Gartner, Hans, "Jewish All-day Schools in Belgium" *Jewish Education*, (Summer, 1950).

Gelber, N. M., "Toledoth Beth Hamedrash LeRabanim BeVinah," *Mosedoth Torah B'Eyropah Bevinyanam Ubechurbanam*. New York: Ogen Publishing House of Histadruth Ivrith of America, 1956. Samuel K. Mirsky, Editor.

Gibbons, Herbert Adams, *The Foundation of the Ottoman Empire*. Oxford: Oxford University Press, 1918.

Ginzberg, Louis, *Students, Scholars, and Saints*. Philadelphia: The Jewish Publication Society, 1945.

Goldschmidt, J., "Religious Education in Israel," *Jewish Education*, (Spring, 1958).

Goodblatt, Morris S., *Jewish Life in Turkey in the XVIth Century*. New York: The Jewish Theological Seminary of America, 1952.

Gourari, S., "The Story of the United Lubavitcher Yeshivoth," *Jewish Education* XX (Fall, 1948).

Graetz, Herzl, *History of the Jews*. Philadelphia: The Jewish Publication Society, 1891. Translated from the German by Bella Levy et al.

Grinberg, Shlomo Simon, "Chinuch Dathi," *Encyclopedia Chin???*. Jerusalem: Misrad Hachinuch VeHatarbuth Umosad Bialik, publishers, 1959.

Grinstein, Hyman B., "An Early Parochial School," *Jewish Education*, XIII, 1941.

Guss, Isaac, "Hachinuch HaYivri B'Africa Ha'dromith," *Sheviley Hachinuch* XIX, (Winter, 1959).

Halpern, Israel, *Pinkas Vaad Arba Aratzoth* ("The Council of the Four Lands"). Jerusalem: Mosad Bialik Publishing Company, 1945.

Hartstein, Jacob, I., "The Yeshivah Looks Back over fifty Years, *Jewish Education*, IX (April-June, 1937), pp. 53-57.

Hebrew Teachers Union of New York City and Vicinity, The *Sefer Hayovel shel Agudath Hamorim Hayivrim BeNew York Usevivotov*. To commemorate the thirtieth year of its foundation. New York, 1944.

Hershberg, Avraham Shemuel, *Pinkkos Bialystok* ("The Chronicle of Bialystok"), Source material for the history of the Jews of Bialystok till the period after the first World War. New Bialystok Jewish Historial Association, Inc., Yudel Marx (editor), vols. I, 1949 and II, 1950.

Heschel, Abraham Joshua, "The Eastern European Era in Jewish History," *Yivo Annual of Jewish Social Sciences*. New York, Yiddish Scientific Institute, I, 1946, pp. 86-106.

Higger, M., *Maseket Derek Erets* (Treatise on Ethics). New York, "Debe Rabenau," 1934.

Hirsch, Samson Rafael, *Igroth Tzafon* ("The Nineteen Letters of Ben Uziel"). New York: Funk and Wagnalls Company, 1899. Translated into English by Bernard Drachman.

Histadruth Ivrith of America, *Mosedoth Torah BeEyropah Bevinyanam Uvechurbanam* ("Jewish Institutions of Higher Learning in Europe—Their Development and Destruction"). New York: Ogen Publishing House of Histadruth Yivrith of America, 1956. Samuel K. Mirsky, editor.

Indelman, Elchanan, "Tarbuth' BePolin, Mekorah Vegidulah, Chazonah Vechilyonah," *Hachinuch Vehatarbuth Hayivrith B'Eyropah*. New York: Ogen Publishing House of Histadruth Ivrith of America, 1957. Zevi Scharfstein, Editor.

Jung, Leo, *Essentials of Judaism*. New York: Union of Orthodox Congregations of America, 1953, tenth edition.

Jung, Leo, "Orthodox Judaism," *Judaism*. New York: National Committee on Contemporary Jewish Affairs, National Council of Jewish Women, 1944.

Jungreiss, Itzchak Isaac Halevi, "Yeshivath Chatham Sofer Be Pressburg," *Mosedoth Torah B'Eyropah Bevinyanam Ubechurbanam*. New York: Ogen Publishing House of Histadruth Ivrith of America, 1956.

Kahane, Zalman, "Mifala Hachinuchi shel Hayahaduth Hadathith BePolin," *Hachinuch Vehatarbuth Hayivrith B'Eyropah*. New York: Ogen Publishing House of Histadruth Ivrith of America, 1957. Zevi Scharfstein, Editor.

Kaplan, Mordecai M., *The Future of the American Jew*. New York: The Macmillan Company, 1948.

Karlikov, Abraham, "Belgium," *The American Jewish Yearbook*, LX. New York: The American Jewish Committee, 1959.

Karlikov, Abraham, "France," *The American Jewish Yearbook*, LX. New York: The American Jewish Committee, 1958.

Karlikov, Abraham, "France," *The American Jewish Yearbook*, LX. New York: The American Jewish Committee, 1959.

Karlin, Rabbi Isaac of, *Chidushay Halachoth al Masecheth Yevamoth*. New York: "Halachah" Publishing Company, 1945.

Kayserling, M., "Sephardim," *Jewish Encyclopedia*, XI, New York: Funk and Wagnalls Company, 1905.

Kohn, Pinchas Jacob, "Caro, Joseph," *The Universal Jewish Encyclopedia*, III. New York: Universal Jewish Encyclopedia Co. Inc., 1941.

Korey, Harold, "The Story of Jewish Education in Chicago," *Jewish Education*, 1954.

Landau, Bezalel P. I., *Introduction, Sh'eloth U'Teshuvoth Beth Yosef*. Jerusalem: Tifereth Hatorah, Publisher, 1960.

Lauterbach, J. Z., "Mishnah," *The Jewish Encyclopedia*, VIII. New York: Funk and Wagnalls Company, 1905, pp. 609-618.

Levitz, Jacob, "Jewish Education in Mexico," *Jewish Education* XXVI, (Spring, 1956).

Lewis, H., "Jewish Education in London," *Jewish Education* X, (April-June, 1938).

Macalister, R.A.S., *A History of Civilization in Palestine*. London: Cambridge University Press, 1912.

Maimonides (Rabbi Moses ben Maimon), *Sefer Iggereth Teshuvath Ramba'M Za'L* ("A Collection of Maimonides' Letters"). Konigsberg: Albert Rosbach, 1819. A letter of Maimonides to Rabbi Pinchas Bar Meshulam of Alexandria, pp. 35-44.

Mandel, Arnold, "France," *The American Jewish Yearbook*, LXII. New York: The American Jewish Committee, 1961.

Maintz, Ernest, *Les Juifs d'Alger sous la Domination Turque*, reprint from *Journal Asiatique*. Paris: Imprimerie National, 1952.

Maller, Julius B., "The Role of Education in Jewish History," *The Jews*. New York: Harper and Brothers, 1945.

Marcus, Jacob Radir, *The Jew in the Medieval World—A Source Book, 315-1791*. Cincinnati: The Union of American Hebrew Congregations, 1938.

Margolis, Max L., and Marx, Alexander, *A History of the Jewish People*. Philadelphia: The Jewish Publication Society of America, 1937.

Meites, H. L., *History of the Jews in Chicago*. Chicago: Jewish Historical Society of Illinois, 1924.

Michael, J., "Beth Hamedrash Lerabanim Bevarshah," *Mosedoth Torah B'Eyropah Bevinyanam Ubechurbanam*. New York: Ogen Publishing House of Histadruth Ivrith of America, 1956.

Mielziner, M., *Introduction to the Talmud*. New York: Bloch Publishing company, Inc., 1925. Third Edition.

Mizrachi Education Committee., *Hachinuch Shel Hamizrachi Baaretz*. Jerusalem: Keren Eretz Israel shel Hamizrachi, 1940.

Montgomery, Mary W., "Turkey," *Jewish Encyclopedia* XII. New York: Funk and Wagnalls Company, 1906.

Nachmanides (Rabbi Mosheh ben nachman), *Kol Chidushay Haramba'n al Talmud Habavli*. B'nei Berak: "Kulmus" Givatayim Publishing Company, 1959.

Nakritz, Yehudah Leib, "Yeshivoth Novardok," in Mosedoth Torah BeEyropah BeVinyanam Ve'Churbanam. New York: Ogen Publishing House of Histadruth Yivrith of America, 1956, pp. 247-290.

Neuman, Abraham A., *The Jews in Spain*. Philadelphia: The Jewish Publication Society of America, 1942.

Nobel, Shlomo, "The Image of the American Jew in Hebrew and Yiddish Literature in America, 1870-1900," *Yivo Annual of Jewish Social Studies* IX, 1954.

Orland, E.M., "West Germany," *The American Jewish Yearbook*, LXI. New York: The American Jewish Committee, 1960.

Orland, E.M., "West Germany," *The American Jewish Yearbook*, IXII. New York: The American Jewish Committee, 1961.

Pilch, Judah, *Jewish Education Register and Directory*. New York: American Association for Jewish Education, 1951.

Poliakov, Leon, "France," *American Jewish Yearbook*, LXI. New York: American Jewish Committee.

Rabenu Asher ben Yechiel (Ra''SH), *Piskay Harash*, appended to *Talmud Bavli*. New York: Otzar Hasefarim, 1958.

Rabenu Nissim (RA''N), *Ra'n al hari'E*. New York: M'Oroth Publishing Company, 1960.

RaSHB'A (Rabbi Shelomo ben Adret), *Sofer Chidushay HaRaSHB'A*. New York: Arieh Leib Reinman, Publisher, 1952.

Rieger, Eliezer, *Hachinuch Hayivri B'Eretz Israel, Yesodoth Umegamoth*. Tel Aviv: "Dvir" Publishing Company, Ltd., 1940.

Rosenberg, Louis, "Canada," *The American Jewish Yearbook*, LIX. New York: The American Jewish Committee, 1958.

Rosenberg, Louis, "Canada," *The American Jewish Yearbook*, LX. New York: The American Jewish Committee, 1959.

Rosenberg, Louis, "Latin America," *The American Jewish Yearbook*, LX. New York: The American Jewish Committee, 1959.

Rosenfeld, Leonard, "Jewish Education in Iran," *Jewish Education*, XXXI, 1961.

Rosenthal, Yehudah, "Beth Hamedrash LeRabanim BeBerlin," *Mosedoth Torah B'Eyropah*. New York: Ogen Publishing House of Histadruth Ivrith of America, 1956.

Roth, Cecil, *The History of the Jews in Italy*. Philadelphia: The Jewish Publication Society, 1946.

Roth, Cecil, "The European Age in Jewish History," *The Jews*. New York: Harper and Brothers, 1949. Louis Finkelstein, editor. Vol. I.

Roth, Cecil, "The Jews of Western Europe," *The Jews*. New York: Harper and Brothers, 1949. Louis Finkelstein, editor.

Ruzanis, Shlomo, *Divray Yemay Israel Bethograma—1300-1520*, ("The History of the Jews in Turkey—1300-1520"). Tel Aviv: "Dvir" Publishing Company, Ltd., 1930.

Sapir, Boris, "The Soviet Union," *The American Jewish Yearbook*, LX. New York: The American Jewish Committee, 1959.

Sapir, Boris, "West Germany," *The American Jewish Yearbook*, LIX. New York: The American Jewish Committee, 1958.

Sapir, Boris, "West Germany," *The American Jewish Yearbook*, LX. New York: The American Jewish Committee, 1959.

Scharfstein, Zevi, *Hachinuch B'Eretz Israel*. New York: Ogen Publishing Company, 1928.

Scharfstein, Zevi, *History of Jewish Education in Modern Times, Europe 1789-1914*, Vol. I. New York: Ogen Publishing company, 1945.

Scharfstein, Zevi, *Toledoth Hachinuch BeIsrael Bedoroth Haacharonim* ("History of Jewish Education in Modern times"). New York: Ogen Publishing company, 1947.

Schechter, Solomon, *Studies in Judaism*, Second Series. Philadelphia: The Jewish Publication Society, 1908.

Segal, Samuel M., *Jewish Elementary All-Day Schools in the City of New York through 1948*, thesis, New York University School of Education, Number ID 3907.E3, 1952, S4, July 2, 1952.

Seidman, Leonard, "Belgium," *The American Jewish Yearbook*, LXII. New York: The American Jewish Committee, 1961.

Shapiro, Leon, "Soviet Union," *The American Jewish Yearbook*, LIX. New York: The American Jewish Committee, 1958.

Shapiro, Leon, "Soviet Union," *The American Jewish Yearbook*, LXI. New York: The American Jewish Committee, 1960.

Shapiro, Leon, "Soviet Union," *The American Jewish Yearbook*, LXII. New York: The American Jewish Committee, 1961.

Shatzky, Jacob, *Yiddishe Bildungs Politik in Polin fun 1806 bis 1866* ("Jewish Educational Policies in Poland between 1806-1866"). New York: Yiddish Scientific Institute, 1943.

Shiff, Murray, "Canada," *American Jewish Yearbook*, LXI. New York: The American Jewish Committee, 1960.

Shill, Yuda Leib, *Sefer Minhagay Baal Hachatham Sofer*, Second Edition. Erlau: Tzeirei Agudath Israel Publishers, 1950.

Shulvass, Mosheh Avigdor, "Beth Hamedrash Lerabanim BeBerlin," *Mosedoth Torah B'Eyropah BeVinyanam Ubechurbanam*. New York: Ogen Publishing House of Histadruth Ivrith of America, 1956.

Silver, Louis, "The Jews in Albany, New York—1655-1914," *Yivo Annual of Jewish Social Science*, IX, 1954.

Shatsky, Yaacov, "Geschichte fun Bildung un Derzihung bei Yidn," *Yivo*, VII. Vilna, 1933.

Shtern, Yekhiel, "Heyder and Bais-Medresh," *Yivo Bletter*, XXXI-XXXII, 1948, pp. 37-130.

Sversky, Aaron, *Introduction, Maggid Maysharim*. Jerusalem: "Orah" Publishing Company, 1960.

Temkin, Sefton D., "Great Britain," *The American Jewish Yearbook*, LIX. New York: The American Jewish Committee, 1958.

Temkin, Sefton D., "Great Britain," *The American Jewish Yearbook*, LX. New York: The American Jewish Committee, 1959.

Temkin, Sefton D., "Great Britain," *The American Jewish Yearbook*, LXI. New York: The American Jewish Committee, 1960.

Temkin, Sefton D., "Great Britain," *The American Jewish Yearbook*, LXII. New York: The American Jewish Committee, 1961.

Toynbee, Arnold J., *Turkey, a Past and a Future*. New York: George H. Doran Company, 1919.

Valentine, Hugo, "Belgium," *The American Jewish Yearbook*, LIX. New York: The American Jewish Committee, 1958.
Valentine, Hugo, "The Scandinavian Countries and Finland," *The American Jewish Yearbook*, LIX. New York: The American Jewish Committee, 1958.
Valentine, Hugo, "Scandinavia and Finland," *The American Jewish Yearbook*, LXI. New York: The American Jewish Committee, 1960.
Waxman, Meyer, *A History of Jewish Literature*. New York: Bloch Publishing Company, 1943.
Waxman, Nissan, *Appendix to Tomer Deborah* by Moses Cordovero. New York: Shoshanim Publishing company, 1960.
Weingarten, David, "Yeshivath Etz Chayim DeHeyda," *Mosedoth Torah B'Eyropah BeVinyanam Ubechurbanam*. New York: Ogen Publishing House of Histadruth Yivrith of America, 1956.
Wishnitzer, Mark, "Chomer Letoledoth Hayeshivoth B'Eyropah Hamizrachith Beshnoth 1919-1939," *Talpioth*, V (December, 1950).
Wishnitzer, Mark, "The Restoration of the Eastern European Yeshivoth after World War I," *Yivo Bletter*, XXXI-XXXII, 1948.
Wolf 2nd, Edwin, and Whiteman, Maxwell, *the History of the jews of Philadelphia from Colonial Times to the age of Jackson*. Philadelphia: The Jewish Publication Society of America, 1957.
Yaavetz, Z'ev, *Toledoth Israel* ("The History of the Jews"). Tel Aviv: "Achiever" Publisher, 1937.
Yosef (Rabbi) ben Meyir, *Peri Megadim*, appended to *Shulchan Aruch Orach Chayim*, part I. New York: Mofitzay Torah Publishing Company, 1951.
Zachs, Nissan, *Haerez MeVilna*, ("Rabbi Shelomoh Zalman of Volozin"). Jerusalem: "Kinor David" Publisher, 1957.
Zeidman, Hillel, "Yeshivoth Kether Torah Meyisudo shel HaRabbi Meradomsk," *Mosedoth Torah B'Eyropah BeVinyanam Ubechurbanam*. New York: Ogen Publishing House of Histadruth Ivrith of America, 1956.
Zeidman, Hillel, "Yeshivoth Lubavitch," *Mosedoth Torah B'Eyropah BeVinyanam Ubechurbanam*. New York: Ogen Publishing House of Histadruth Yivrith of America, 1956.
Zamba, Abraham, "Methivtah BeVarsha," *Mosedoth Torah B'Eyropah BeVinyanam Ubechurbanam*. New York: Ogen Publishing House of Histadrut Ivrith of America, 1956.
Zimberg, Israel, *Di Geschichte fun di Literatur bei Idn*. New York: Farlag Morris S. Sklarsky, 1943.

B. CURRICULA AND PERTINENT PUBLICATIONS

Associated Talmud Torahs of Chicago, *Tochnith Halimudim Lechamesh Shenoth Limud BeTalmud Torah*, ("A Talmud Torah Curriculum"). Chicago: January, 1960.
Avigail, M., "Tochnith Halimudim BeVeit Hasefer HeYesodi Beyisrael," *Fundamental Principles for Diaspora Education*, Proceedings of Institute on Diaspora Education held under the auspices of the Jewish Agency at Zofith, Israel, August 14-18, 1955.
Avigail, M., "Tochnith Halimudim Lekitoth Beit-Gimmel," (The Program of Study for

Grades B and C), *Madrich Lekitoth Beth-Gimmel*. Tel Aviv: Havaad Hapoel-Merkaz Letarbuth Ulechinuch, Hahistadruth Hakelalith shel Haovidim Hayivrim B'Eretz Israel, 1958.

Board of Education of the City of New York, *Curriculum Development in the Elementary Schools*. New York: Curriculum Bulletin No. 1, 1955-56 series, 1955. William Jansen, Superintendent of Schools.

Bortnikker, Elijah, in cooperation with The Principals' Council Board of Education, Metropolitan Council, United Synagogue, *Outline of Studies for the First Year of the Congregational Hebrew School*. New York: Jewish Education Committee of New York, 1957. Dedicated to the memory of Leon Kohn.

Commission on Jewish Education of the Union of American-Hebrew Congregations and the Central Conference of American Rabbis, *An Outline of the Curriculum of the Jewish Religious School*. New York: The Union of American Hebrew Congregations, 1959-60. Eugene B. Borowitz, editor. Dedicated to Dr. Emanual Gamorah.

Desler, N.Z., *Tochnith Halimudim, 1959 Beith Chinuch Hayivri*. Cleveland: Torah Umesorah Publishers, 1959.

Dushkin, Alexander M., and Engelman, Uriah Z., *Report of Commision for the Study of Jewish Education in the United States* New York: American Association for Jewish Education, 1959.

Fendel, Zachary, *Yeshivah Preparatory High School, Forest Hills, L.I. Bulletin of General Information*. New York: 1959.

Frishberg, I.Z., *Tochnith Limudim Kelalith Lemosedoth Hachinuch Haamameim*. New York: Mizrachi National Education Committee, 1946.

Gamoran, Emanual (ed.), *A Curriculum for the Jewish Religious Schools*. Cincinnati: Union of American Hebrew Congregations, 1946-1947.

Hebrew Culture Service Committee, *Hebrew in Colleges and Universities*. New York: Hebrew Culture Service Committee for American High Schools and Colleges, 1958. Judah Lapson, editor.

Hebrew Union College-Jewish Institute of Religion, *Catalogue*, 1958-1959-1960.

Hurley, Beatrice Davis, *curriculum for Elementary School Children;* New York: The Ronald Press Company, 1959.

Jewish Theological Seminary of America, *Register*. New York: 1958.

Jews's Cllege—London, *Hundred and Third Annual Report*. London: 1960.

Machleket Hachinuch shel HaSochnuth HaYehudith L'Eretz Israel, *Tochnith Halimudim Hanehugah Bevatey Sefer shel Hamizrachi*, IX. Jerusalem, 1932.

"Merkos L'Inyonei Chinuch," *Tochnith Limudim A. Lemosedoth Chinuch Lenarim B. Levotei Sefer Lenaaroth* (A Program of Study for Boys' Schools and for Girls' Schools). New York: Merkos L'Inyonei Chinuch, Inc., Publishers, 1944.

Misred Hachinuch Vehatarbuth, *Tochnith Halimudim Leveith Hasefer Hayesodi Hamamlachti Hadathi, Grade Four*. Jerusalem: Government Printing Press, Tishri, 1957.

New York University *School of Education Bulletin*, LXI, May 15, 1961. New York Univeristy, 1961-1962.

New York University *School of Education Announcement*, 1961-1962.

Outline of Studies for the Second Year of the Congregational School. New York: Jewish Education Committee of New York, 1960. Dedicated to the Memory of Lillie Rubee.

Principals Council, The Associated United Synagogue Schools in Queens, *Course of Studies for Second Year*. New York: The Jewish Education Committee of New York, Inc., 1951.

Principals Council, *Course of Studies for Third Year*. New York: Jewish Education Committee of New York, Inc., 1951.

Principals Council, *Course of Studies for Fourth Year*. New York: Jewish Education Committee of New York, Inc., 1951.

Ruffman, Louis L., in cooperation with the Committee on Objectives, Standards and Curricula of the United Synagogue Commission on Jewish Education, and, with the assistance of Abraham Segel, *Curriculum Outline for the congregational School* (revised edition). New York: United Synagogue Commission on Jewish Education, 1959.

Union of American Hebrew Congregations, *A Curriculum for the Jewish Religious School*. Cincinnati: 1946-1947.

Vaad Hatochnith shel Agudath Hamnahlim Hayivrim, *Tochnith Limudim Levotei HaTalmud Torah* (Second Edition, Part I). New York: Jewish Publication Committee of New York, Inc., Menachem M. Edelstein, editor, 1950.

Yeshiva University Bulletin, *Stern College for Women, Catalogue 1959-61*. New York: 1959.

Yeshiva University *Bulletin of General Information*, VII, (September, 1959).

IV Texts of the Shulchan Aruch

Danzig, Abraham, *Chokamath Adam—Shulchan Aruch Yoreh Deah*. Stettin: A Strentzel, Publisher, 1861.

Feldman, David, *Kitzur Shulchan Aruch*. Leipzig: David Feldman, Publisher, 1924.

Ganzfried, Shelomoh, *Kitzur Shulchan Aruch al Hilchoth Pesach*. Lodz: "Sefer" Publishing Company, third edition (no date given).

Caro, Joseph, *Shulchan Aruch Choshen Mishpat*. Amsterdam: Hertz Levy and Kashman, Publishers, 1748.

Caro, Joseph, *Shulchan Aruch Even Haezer*. Amsterdam: Kashman, Publisher, 1770. Third Edition.

Caro, Joseph, *Shulchan Aruch Even Haezer*. Amsterdam, Yochanan Levy and Company, Publishers, 1785. Fourth Edition.

Caro, Joseph, *Shulchan Aruch Orach Chayim*. Dichrenfurth: Yosef Mayo, Publisher, 1866.

Caro, Joseph, *Shulchan Aruch Orach Chayim*. Amsterdam: Yosef Props, Publisher, 1775.

Balaban, Hessel, *Shulchan Aruch Yoreh Deah*, Part II. Lemberg: Pessel Balaban, Publisher, 1888.

Caro, Joseph, *Shulchan Aruch Yoreh Deah*. Amsterdam: Abraham Solomon Props, 1778.

Caro, Joseph, *Shulchan Aruch*. Cracow: Rabbi Mosheh ben Itzchak Yehudah Liva in cooperation with the Vaad Arba Aratzoth, Publishers, 1670.

Caro, Yosef, *Shulchan Aruch*. New York: Chananiah Yomtov Lipa Goldman, Publisher, 1953.

Caro, Joseph, *Shulchan Aruch Chosen Mishpat*. Lublin: Rabbi Shabethai Cohen (Sha'ch), in cooperation with the Vaad Arba Aratzoth, 1654.

Caro, Joseph, *Shulchan Aruch-Chosen Mishpat, Shulchan Aruch-Yoreh Deah*, Lemberg; Druck v. verlag, Pessel Balaban, 1864. *Shulchan Aruch Chosen Mishpat*. Lemberg: Druck v. verlag Pessel Balaban, 1898. *Even Haezer*. Lemberg: Druck v. verlag, Pessel Balaban, 1886.

Caro, Joseph, *Shulchan Aruch*. Part I, *Orach Chayim*. Lemberg: A. J. Madfes, 1876. Part II, *Yoreh Deah*. Lemberg: A. J. Madfes, 1876. Part III, *Even Haezer*. New York: Mosheh Chayim Pollack, 1946. Part IV, *Choshen Mishpat*. Lemberg, A. J. Madfes, 1876.

Code of Jewish Law (four volumes), Hyman C. Goldin, Editor. New York: Hebrew Publishing Company, 1927.

Danzig, Abraham, *Chayei Adam al Shulchan Aruch Orach Chayim*. Vilna: A. Z. Schriftzetzer and M. M. Rosenkrantz, Publishers, 1895.

Danzig, Abraham ben Yechiel, *Chayye Adam*, and *Hokmat Adam*. Vilna: Schriftsetzer, Publisher, 1895.

Denburg, Chayim N., *Code of Hebrew Law—Shulchan Aruch Yoreh Deah*. Montreal: The Jurisprudence Press, 1954.

Feldman, David, *Kitzur Shulchan Aruch*. New York: Fourth Edition, 1947.

Ganzfried, Shelomoh, *Kitzur Shulchan Aruch*, New York. New York: Hebrew Publishing Company, 1927.

Ganzfried, Shelomo, *Sefer Kitzur Shulchan Aruch Hashalem*. jerusalem: Eshkol Publishing, 1954.

Goldin, Hyman E., *The Jew and His Duties*, The Essence of the Kitzur Shulchan Aruch Ethically Presented. New York: Hebrew Publishing Company, 1953.

Goldin, H. E., *Code of Jewish law*. New York: Hebrew Publishing Company, 1960. (Hebrew-English).

Goldin, H. E., *shulchan Aruch shel Kis*, ("Pocket Size Shulchan Aruch"). New York: Hebrew Publishing Company, 1960.

Kagan, Israel Meir Hacohen, *Mishnah Berurah—A Commentary on the Shulchan Aruch Orach Chayim*. Jerusalem: Torah Laam Publishing, 1960.

Löwe, Heinrich George L., (translator), *Der Shulchan Aruch*. Hamburg: Perthes-Besser and Manke, 1837.

Luria, Rabenu Itzchak, *Shulchan Aruch, Mystic Interpretation*. Warsaw: Leib Rosenblatt, Publisher, 1881.

Reinman, L., *Shulchan Aruch Orach Chayim*, Part I. New York: L. Reinman, Publisher, 1951.

Shneur, Zalman, *Shulchan Aruch*. Vilna: Fradel Metz, Publisher, 1904.

V. School Texts of the Shulchan Aruch.

Applebaum, Yosef, *Peninay Hadath-Meain Shulchan Aruch Sheetsti Umeforash Lahavonath Hatalmidim*, ("Pearls of the Religion—A Shulchan Aruch-like Compendium for Students"). New York: A. L. Frankel, Publisher, 1958. (See also, Bloch Publishing Company, 1961.

Ben Ezra, A., *Shavuoth, Laws and customs . . . Prayers*. New York: The Mizrachi National Education Committee, 1950.

Ben Ezra, A., *Yamim Norayim Vesukkoth* ("High Holy Days and Sukkoth") . . . Laws, Customs and Prayers. New York: The Mizrachi National Education Committee, 1950.

Bialik, Manoach L., *Shabbath* . . . Discusses laws of Sabbath . . . Prayers. New York: The Mizrachi National Education Committee, 1950.

Bloch Publishing company, *commandments, Creeds and Holidays*. For use in Jewish Religious Schools. New York: 1932. Thirty-fifth Thousand—contains prayers and blessings.

Bogaisky, S., *Dinay Israel Uminhagav Vethamayhem*, "Jewish Laws and Customs"), illustrated. New York: Bloch Publishing Company, 1961.

Bogaisky, S., *Orach Israel* ("Israel's Way of Life"). New York: Bloch Publishing Company, 1928.

Konovitz, Israel, *Dinim Uminhagim al pi Kitzur Shulchan Aruch*, ("Laws and Customs Based on the Kitzur Shulchan Aruch"). New York: Bloch Publishing Company, 1961.

Curriculum Committee of the Hebrew Principals' Association of New York, in cooperation with the Jewish Education Committee of New York, *Reshith Hokhma* ("The Beginning of Wisdom"), a little book of prayers, blessings, and hymns for Jewish Children. New York: Hebrew Publishing Company, 1941.

Eisenstein, Yehudah David, *shulchan Aruch Orach Chayim—Hilchoth berochoth* ("The Code of Life", Part I—Benedictions of the Shulchan Aruch-Orach Chayim . . . Rearranged and translated. New York: J. Aronson Press, 1900.

Friedman, David Aryeh, *Shulchan Aruch Levnay Hanevrim* ("The shulchan Aruch for the Young"). New York: Hebrew Publishing Company, 1960.

Goldin, Ch. A., *Code of Jewish Law* (School text in English). New York: Hebrew Publishing company, 1960.

Greenstein, Joseph, *Shavuos* ("Feast of Weeks") . .How We Observe Shavuos. . . . New York: The Mizrachi National Education Committee, 1950.

Guttmacher, Adolph, *A Sabbath School Companion* for Jewish Children. New York: Bloch Publishing Company, Inc., 1926. Contains Biblical stories, benedictions, and dietary laws. Sixteenth thousand.

Hurwitz, S. I., *Shulchan Aruch LeTalmudim*, ("Shulchan Aruch for Students"). New York: Bloch Publishing Company, 1961.

Hurwitz, Shemariahu Leib Halevi, *Sefer Dinay Israel Uminhagav Leyamim Noroyim*, ("Laws and Customs of Israel for the High Holy Days"). New York: CHinuch Publishing Company, 1924.

Hurwitz, Shemariahu Leib, *Shulchan Aruch LeTalmidim im Agadoth Nivcharoth Mehatalmud Vehamedrashim* ("Shulchan Aruch for Students, with selected excerpts from the Talmud and Medrashim"). New York: Hebrew Publishing Company, 1919.

Hurwitz, Shemariahu Leib, *Shulchan Aruch LeTalmidim*. New York: "Nehemiah" Publishing, 1919 (fourth edition). Reprinted by Hebrew Publishing Company, 1960.

Jacobs, George, *The Hebrew Faith—A Catechism*—For elementary instruction in the Hebrew Faith. New York: Bloch Publishing Company (no date given).

Konovitz, Israel, *Chayai Hayehudi al pi Hashulchan Aruch* ("Life of the Jew According to the Shulchan Aruch"). Based on the Kitzur Shulchan Aruch by Shelomo Ganzfried. New York: "Masoreth" Publishing, 1929.

Levner, I. B., *shulchan Aruch* (abridged and prepared for the school and cheder). New York: S. Srebrek, Publisher, 1924. First printing, Vilna (no dates given). Second Printing, Warsaw (no dates given).

Levner, I. B., *Yedideinu*—discusses the most important festivals, feasts, and prayers needed for children who begin to learn prayers. Warsaw: "Tuchna" Publishing Company, 1903. Second edition has linear translation in Russian.

Orenstein, Frankel, *Shulchan Aruch Layeladim* (English title: "The Torah as our Guide"). New York: Hebrew Publishing Company, 1960.

Rabinowitz, A. Z., *Shulchan Aruch Leyeladim*, ("A Shulchan Aruch for Children"). New York: Star Hebrew Book Company, 1928. Reprinted 1960 by Hebrew Publishing Company.

Shulman, Mosheh I., *Hilchoth Chag Hapasach Lebotei Sefer VeLaam*. The Mizrachi National Educational Committee, Publishers, 1950.

Star Hebrew Book Company, *Shulchan Aruch Leyeladim* ("A Shulchan Aruch for the Childrne"), in two parts. New York: 1928. Appended is *Chinuch Hamidoth* ("Character Education") by M. M. Zalmanowitz.

Weinstein, Deborah, *Chamishah Asar Bishvat*, . . . Customs. New York: The Mizrachi National Education Committee, 1950.

Weinstein, Deborah, *Chanukah—Its Laws and Customs*. New York: The Mizrachi National Education Committee, 1950.